THE FUTURE OF FISCAL POLICY
A REASSESSMENT

C|84

THE FUTURE
OF FISCAL POLICY

•

A REASSESSMENT

Inaugural Lecture, G. Eyskens-leerstoel

by

Richard A. Musgrave

H.H. Burbank Professor of Political Economy / Harvard University

LEUVEN UNIVERSITY PRESS
1978

336
M98 fu

De met de naam van Professor Dr. Gaston Eyskens verbonden publicaties verschijnen onder de auspiciën van de naar hem geheten Leerstoel. Deze Leerstoel is opgericht geworden ter gelegenheid van zijn emeritaatsviering op 4 oktober 1975 en beoogt het onderwijs op het gebied van de theoretische en de toegepaste economie te bevorderen.

Het benaarstigen van dit doel werd mogelijk gemaakt dank zij het fonds dat talrijke instellingen en verenigingen in den lande, hetzij als leden-stichters van de Leerstoel, hetzij als steunverleners, bereid waren te vormen als uiting van hun hoge waardering voor de academische loopbaan die Professor Dr. Gaston Eyskens gedurende een vierenveertigjarig leerambt heeft vervuld.

De Leerstoel Gaston Eyskens wordt beheerd door een Comité van vijf hoogleraren, gekozen onder de leden van de Faculteitsraad der Economische en Toegepaste Economische Wetenschappen van de Katholieke Universiteit te Leuven. Zijn Statuten bepalen dat op initiatief van het Beheerscomité, zo mogelijk om de twee jaar, lezingen, conferenties of gastcolleges zullen worden ingericht, waartoe vooraanstaande vakgenoten uit het binnen- of buitenland als titularissen zullen worden aangezocht. Op voorstel van het Beheerscomité zullen deze wetenschappelijke activiteiten kunnen aanleiding geven tot gedrukte publicaties, die door hun verspreiding er zullen toe bijdragen de naam van Professor Dr. Gaston Eyskens levendig te houden.

Geboren op 1 april 1905 is Gaston Eyskens sinds 1931 aan de Katholieke Universiteit verbonden geweest en heeft hij aan een ongemeen groot aantal studerenden, behorende tot diverse studierichtingen, een gedegen onderricht verschaft op de terreinen van de algemene economie, de publieke financiën en de macro-economische theorie. In de ontwikkeling van zijn Universiteit vindt hij erkenning als grondlegger van het nederlandstalig economie-onderwijs te Leuven.

Uit zijn gevuld curriculum weze nog vermeld, dat hij de gezagsvolle promotor is geweest van het Centrum voor Economische Studiën, dat als researchafdeling bij het Departement Economie van zijn Faculteit einde 1955 is opgericht geworden. Voorts is hij van 1954 tot 1968 lid geweest van de Raad van Beheer van de Katholieke Universiteit. Aan haar maatschappelijke, dienstverlenende taak heeft hij daarenboven een belangrijke dimensie weten te verlenen. Als lid van de Nationale Vergaderingen en als Minister en Regeringsleider is hij een markant dienaar geweest van de idealen van de christelijke sociale arbeidersbeweging in België.

Professor Dr. M. Loeys
Voorzitter Beheerscomité

The "Professor Dr. Gaston Eyskens Lectures" are published under the auspices of the Chair established on the occasion of the promotion of Professor Doctor Gaston Eyskens to Professor Emeritus on 4 October 1975 and named after him. This Chair is intended to promote the teaching of theoretical and applied economics.

The pursuance of this goal is made possible through an endowment fund established by numerous Belgian institutions and associations as an expression of their great appreciation of the long and fruitful teaching career of Professor Gaston Eyskens.

The "Gaston Eyskens Chair of Economics" is administered by a committee of five professors chosen from the members of the Council of the Faculty of Economic and Applied Economic Sciences of the *Katholieke Universiteit te Leuven*. The objective of this Committee is to organize biennially a series of lectures to be given by outstanding scholars. On the recommendation of the Committee, these lectures shall be published to honor the name of Professor Gaston Eyskens.

Born on 1 April 1905, Gaston Eyskens has taught at the Catholic University of Leuven since 1931. For an unusually large number of student generations Professor Eyskens has been the inspiring teacher of general economics, public finance, and macro-economic theory. In the development of his University, he is recognized as the founder of Dutch language economic education in Leuven. His influence on the cultural and economic emancipation of the Flemish community has been enormous.

It should also be mentioned that he was a founder of the Center for Economic Studies of the Department of Economics. He was also a member of the Governing Board of the University from 1954 to 1968, and he succeeded in adding an important dimension to the social service task of the University. As Member of Parliament, Minister, and Head of Government, he dominated the Belgian political scene for many years.

Professor Dr. M. Loeys
Chairman of the Administrative
Committee "Gaston Eyskens
Chair of Economics"

CONTENTS

Growth of the Public Sector

Economic historians of this century will record the growth of the public sector as one of the striking developments of that period. While details and timing differ between countries, the economies of Western Europe and North America have shared a surprisingly uniform pattern of public sector growth. Three dominant characteristics prevail throughout:

1. At the beginning of the century, government expenditures typically ranged from 10 to 15 percent of GNP, but by the mid seventies the expenditure ratios had tripled, reaching from 35 to 45 or even 50 percent. Belgium, I note, stands at the upper end, though not at the top of the scale.

2. As part of this overall expansion, the expenditure composition shifted from purchases to transfers. While the ratio of government purchases to GNP typically doubled, rising from around 10 to 20 percent, the transfer ratio increased ten fold climbing from about 1 to 10 percent. As a result, the typical share of transfers in total expenditures rose from 10 to 30, or, in some cases, 50 percent.

3. Notwithstanding the belligerent nature of our century, military expenditures, it appears, were not the main cause of public sector expansion. Viewed in functional terms, the main increase was in expenditures directed at a variety of "human services", including mostly social security, welfare and education. Such outlays typically rose from around 25 to well over 50 percent of total expenditures, with the share of general government and defense showing a decline. Such was the case especially with the accentuated rate of growth which occurred during the sixties and early seventies.

Table 1

GROWTH OF PUBLIC EXPENDITURES IN THE UNITED STATES*

As % of GNP	1900	1937	1950	1975
Defense	1.5	1.2	8.3	5.5
Social Welfare & Education	1.8	3.0	5.8	19.0
Other	4.0	6.2	9.0	10.5
Total	7.3	10.4	23.1	35.0
Purchases	5.0	7.2	13.5	22.3
Transfers	1.3	1.6	5.0	11.5
Interest	1.0	1.6	1.7	1.2
Total	7.3	10.4	23.1	35.0
As % of Expenses				
Defense	20.8	11.5	36.0	15.9
Social Welfare & Education	24.7	28.8	33.5	54.3
Other	54.5	69.7	30.5	29.8
Total	100.0	100.0	100.0	100.0
Purchases	77.8	69.2	58.4	63.8
Transfers	22.1	15.4	21.6	32.8
Interest	.1	15.4	1.0	3.4
Total	100.0	100.0	100.0	100.0

* Based on R.A. and P.B. Musgrave, *Public Finance in Theory and Practice*, Sec. D., pp. 133-138.

Table 2

GROWTH OF PUBLIC EXPENDITURES IN GERMANY*

As % of GNP	1913	1925	1950	1970
Defense	3.4	3.3	5.6	2.8
Social Welfare & Education	5.1	10.5	14.6	17.7
Other	4.9	6.8	7.9	10.2
Total	13.4	20.6	28.1	30.7
Purchases	10.1	14.2	17.4	19.5
Transfers	1.3	5.9	9.8	8.8
Interest	2.0	.5	.9	2.5
Total	13.4	20.6	28.1	30.8
As % of Expenses				
Defense	25.2	16.0	20.1	9.2
Social Welfare & Education	37.9	51.1	51.8	57.7
Other	36.9	32.9	28.1	33.1
Total	100.0	100.0	100.0	100.0
Purchases	75.3	69.1	62.0	63.4
Transfers	10.0	28.8	35.0	28.7
Interest	14.7	2.1	3.0	7.9
Total	100.0	100.0	100.0	100.0

* Based on R.A. Musgrave, P.B. Musgrave, L. Kullmer, *Die Öffentlichen Finanzen in Theorie und Praxis*, J.C.B. Mohr, Vol. 1, pp. 175-178. Transfers as percent of total expenditures are assumed to equal item 16 plus 1/2 of item 17 (op. cit. 1976) with purchases derived as residual. In arriving at the GNP ratios for 1913, the ratio of GNP to national income is assumed to be the same as that for 1925.

Table 3

As % of GNP	1900	1928	1950	1975
Defense	6.9	2.8	7.2	5.5
Social Welfare & Education	2.6	9.6	18.0	28.5
Other	4.9	11.8	13.8	23.9
Total	14.4	24.2	39.0	57.9
Purchases	13.0	12.0	22.0	24.3
Transfers	.4	5.5	12.6	28.7
Interest	1.0	6.7	4.4	4.9
Total	14.4	24.2	39.0	57.9

As % of Expenses	1900	1928	1950	1975
Defense	48.0	11.4	18.5	9.5
Social Welfare & Education	18.0	39.7	46.3	49.4
Other	34.0	48.9	35.2	41.1
Total	100.0	100.0	100.0	100.0
Purchases	90.3	49.6	56.4	42.8
Transfers	2.7	22.7	32.3	49.5
Interest	7.0	17.7	11.3	7.7
Total	100.0	100.0	100.0	100.0

* Based on Alan T. Peacock and Jack Wiseman, *The Growth of Public Expenditures in the United Kingdom*, Princeton University Press, esp. pp. 71, 190.
For 1975 based on *Annual Abstract of Statistics*, 1976, Central Statistical Office.

What have been the forces behind these surprisingly uniform developments, what are the underlying "laws" of public sector growth and what has been their implication for the structure of modern capitalism? Most important perhaps, will the same trend continue and where will it take us?

1. *Problems of Definition and Measurement*

Before attempting to answer these questions, I must clear the decks by defining how the term "public sector" is to be used in this discussion and how its "growth" is to be measured.

CONCEPT OF PUBLIC SECTOR

While many definitions are possible, our focus will be on the budgetary activity of the public sector, i.e., the provision for public services and transfers, as distinct from public production and the role of public enterprise. Beginning with the provision of public services, the essence of budgetary activity is that such services are made available free of direct charge and financed by tax (or loan) revenue, rather than by fees or price payment. This, of course, is the classical concern of the theory of public finance. Given this focus on budgetary provision, it does not matter whether the goods or services thus provided are produced under public management (e.g., the output of civil servants, or roads constructed by government workers) or whether such output is purchased by government from private firms (e.g., the pencils used by civil servants or roads built by private companies under government contract). By the same token public enterprises, owned by government but selling their products in the market (such as public utilities) are not here considered part of the public sector as they do not involve budgetary provision.

Budgetary provision, or the concept of the public sector as here defined, therefore, must not be confused with public ownership of the means of production. The distinction between public (budgetary) and private provision is not the same as that between socialism and capitalism. A socialist society may choose to withhold factor earnings and to distribute its output free of direct charge, i.e., rely on budgetary provision; or it may pay out factor earnings and distribute goods and services through sale in the market. Similarly, a capitalist society may choose to rely more or less heavily on public provision, with a larger or smaller share of private enterprise output sold to the government. Our concept of budgetary provision may thus be applied to a socialist as well as a capitalist setting.

In rendering public services, budgetary activity requires the transfer of resources from private to public use. The opportunity cost of goods and services which are provided publicly is that fewer resources are left to produce what is available for private purchases. Such is not the case with regard to transfer payments, the other and increasingly important aspect of budgetary provision. Here the final control over incomes stays within the private sector, but is shifted between individuals. This difference renders it awkward to combine government purchases and transfers in a common or overall expenditure ratio. The overall ratio remains meaningful, however, if viewed from the revenue side. It then reflects the share of income which must be diverted to the budget through taxation or borrowing. Viewed in relation to the problems of tax burden, incentive effects and efficiency costs, the implications of a tax dollar are much the same whether it is used to finance purchases or transfers. The overall ratio thus remains meaningful, although there are questions (to be noted presently) of how its denominator should be defined.

By emphasizing this budgetary concept of the public sector, I do not mean to deny that the scope of governmental activity reaches much further. For one thing, our concept of budgetary provision itself is not sharply defined. In particular, there is the question whether government lending should be included as a form of transfer, or whether it should be excluded as a public enterprise (production) activity. Presumably, the answer will depend on whether or not the loan is granted at commercial or subsidized terms. For another, budgetary provision is not the only relevant instrument of economic policy. Non-budgetary forms of activity abound, and in some cases (such as regulation) may serve as a substitute for or supplement to budgetary approaches. While the cost of regulatory agencies enters into the budget, their economic implications can hardly be measured in these terms. In short, non-budgetary aspects of public policy are of great significance, but they are not of primary concern in this discussion.

PROBLEMS OF MEASUREMENT

Having defined our concept of the public sector, a word must be said about how public sector growth is to be measured. Obviously, it is not meaningful to observe that the nominal level of expenditures is now four hundred times as large (using the United States as an example) as it was at the beginning of the century. Surely, a correction must be made for inflation. With current prices about six times those of 1900, expenditures in real terms are only 66 and not 400 times their 1900 level. Next, allowance may be made for the fact that population has more than tripled over the period. Putting the growth of real expenditures on a per capita basis (although we shall see later there is some question about this), the multiple is reduced to 22. Finally, allowance should be made for the fact that per capita income has quadrupled, reflecting productivity gains. Given these gains, it is only reasonable to expect that people will have wished to spend part thereof on publicly rather than privately provided goods and services. It seems reasonable, therefore, to measure growth of the public sector not in absolute terms (even if measured by real per capita expenditures), but as a share in total income or expenditures. Allowing for this, our multiple of 22 is reduced further to about 5. This, of course, is the multiple which may be arrived at directly by dividing the present 35 percent ratio of public expenditures to GNP by the 7 percent ratio which prevailed in 1900.

While there is a clear case for viewing the growth of the public sector in these relative or share terms, I must not leave the impression that this share is easily defined and measured. Difficulties arise not only in combining public purchases with transfers, but also in their aggregation with privately provided goods and services. Where public goods and services are produced by government directly, as with civil service, their inclusion in GNP is at cost, as distinct from the output of private enterprise which is valued so as to include a profit margin. Moreover, a difference exists in that the prices of privately purchased goods and services directly reflect consumer evaluation, whereas the value of publicly provided goods and services (whether produced privately or publicly) has to be validated through the more complex mechanism of a political (voting) process.

Next, there is the question of what to do about changes in relative prices. By focussing on the changing *ratio* of public expenditures to GNP, even though both are measured in nominal terms, the problem of deflating or adjustment for change in price level appears to be taken care of automatically. However, the implicit adjustment is correct only if the prices of publicly and privately provided goods have risen at the same rate. Such may not be the case. Taking the longer view, goods and services provided by government may lend themselves less to technical advances than those privately provided, simply because they are less technology intensive. Thus their relative prices may be expected to rise. Over a shorter period, nominal public sector costs may move at a different rate than private sector prices, be it due to changes in market structure or in demand. The unionization of public employees and rising public sector wages, have been a major factor in recent U.S. experience. While the ratio of government purchases to GNP as measured in current prices rose from 13 to 22 percent over the 1950-75 period, this increase is reduced by two-thirds if numerator and denominator of the ratio are deflated by their respective price indices.

17

Relative price changes may thus be a major factor in interpreting short run developments, but they do not play the same role in the long run view.[1] Moreover, one may question whether relative price changes should be adjusted for. The purpose, after all, is not to measure physical factor inputs or quantities of output, but to measure the value which various components contribute to GNP. Assuming an efficient process of budget determination, provision of public services at a relatively higher cost would seem to reflect that their relative value to the consumer has risen, and this should not be washed out by the deflating process.

Next there is a question of how the denominator of the ratio should be defined. Should one use GNP at market price or at factor cost, or should the comparison be in terms of national income? My inclination is to use GNP at market price where purchases or the total expenditure ratio are concerned, while using net national product at factor cost when dealing with transfer payments or direct taxes. Though significant for cross-country comparisons at a given point of time, this issue loses in importance if focus is on longer term trends. For these and other reasons some care must be taken in interpreting overall public sector growth in terms of Tables 1-3, but the basic trends emerge with sufficient clarity to survive these qualifications.

2. *Causes of Public Sector Growth*

Turning to the causes of public sector growth, one is tempted to argue that such growth is the outcome of political, rather than economic forces. Indeed, there was a time when students of public finance felt that the appropriate size of the public sector was not their concern but should be left to politicians, or at best, to political science. But fortunately such is no longer the case. While the rise of popular democracy and the growth of egalitarian ideology have been a major cause of public sector growth, it remains interesting, nevertheless, to begin with a more economic view of the matter.

THE ECONOMIC RATIONALE OF EXPENDITURE GROWTH

I begin with government purchases which, as noted before, rose from about 10 to 20 percent of GNP. Is this a surprising outcome and how can the theory of social goods contribute to its explanation? To consider the economics of the problem, let me suppose that the budgetary development has reflected an efficient economic process, designed to furnish people with the mix of goods and services – publicly and privately provided – which they wish to obtain in the course of rising incomes. In this case how would we have expected the ratio of public purchases to GNP to have behaved?

Population Growth and Social Goods. To begin with, consider the role of population (as distinct from income) growth. Modern fiscal theory defines social goods as goods which are non-rival in consumption. Such goods cannot be provided effectively through the market. Since exclusion cannot or should not be applied to their provision, people will act as free riders and budget provision (financed by the imposition of taxes) is needed. But if consumption of social goods is non-rival, per capita cost of any given total supply will be less, the larger is the number of consumers. Hence, the relative price of social goods (the tax-price with which the individual taxpayer is confronted) should be expected to fall as numbers increase. If the price elasticity of demand exceeds unity, the share of expenditures directed at such goods will rise. This may help to explain what has happened, but it also suggests that *per capita* growth of GNP understates the resulting welfare gain. However, this reasoning is applicable only to the polar case of pure social goods, and not to that of "mixed goods" the benefit of which are subject to spatial limitations or to congestion. As has been emphasized in the discussion of recent years, such goods make up a significant share of budgetary provision, especially at the local level of government, so that the above argument does not apply.

Consumer goods. Returning to the assumption that budgetary provision is for social goods proper (i.e. goods non-rival in consumption) consider now the implications of growth in per capita income.

Beginning with social goods of the consumer-good type, how would one expect the expenditure ratio to behave? Assuming the relative prices of social and private goods to remain unchanged, the answer now hinges on the income elasticity of demand. Provided they are in the nature of normal goods, outlays on social consumer goods will rise with per capita income. Income elasticity of demand will be positive. But resulting changes in the expenditure ratio will depend on whether demand elasticity is below, at or above unity. Would one expect elasticity to exceed unity or, putting it differently, that social consumption goods as a group tend to be in the nature of luxuries rather than necessities? I find it difficult to answer this question as illustrations of both sorts come to mind. Adam Smith, for instance, emphasized the need for providing public services to the poor, so as to supply them with the essential necessities needed for the maintenance of human dignity. More generally, the basic legal institutions which provide

19

the framework in which society functions are clearly a necessity. But other public services such as education may straddle both categories, while still others such as recreation facilities are clearly of the luxury type. They may be so in their own right or because they are complementary to privately provided luxury goods. As I see it, there is no obvious presumption in either direction, leaving me with the assumption of unit elasticity as a reasonable point of departure.

Public Investment.   Generalizations may be easier to derive when it comes to social capital goods. The question here is whether additions to the capital stock required at various stages of economic development are of the public or the private type. Capital goods, the benefits of which are largely external, such as infra-structure investments, will have to be provided publicly. The canals and roads of Adam Smith as well as their modern counterparts of power facilities and irrigation projects illustrate this need. Others, the benefits of which are clearly internal, such as manufacturing plant or equipment may be provided privately. In some instances, even such investments may carry important linkage effects to economic development and thus involve externalities which call for public support. In all, there is reason to expect that capital formation in the less developed countries will involve a larger public share than that in developed countries. This suggests that the share in total investment based on budgetary provision may be expected to decline as income rises.

Perhaps so, but prediction is precarious especially since random factors such as changes in population growth and technology also enter. Consider for instance the increasing importance of human investment in education. As we have seen, a large part of the increase in government purchases over recent years has been in this area, responding to an increased awareness of the high returns which may be derived as well as to changing demographic factors, especially population growth. Or, consider the importance of technological change. As technology advances, new goods become available, the benefits of which may be externality intensive, and which must therefore be provided by the public sector. Thus the invention of the steam engine called for public provision of rail beds, and the rise of the automobile with the consequent expansion of demand for public highways dominated the development of public purchase expenditures over the last fifty years. Who knows what types of public provision will be called for by the energy or inter-planetary transportation systems of the future?

Defense.   Similar speculations may be applied to defense. Taking a protectionist view of the state function, it might be argued that economic development, by raising the ratio of capital stock to GNP, will call for a rising share of GNP to be diverted to the protection of property. On the other hand, this may be dampened by economies of scale in the cost of rendering protection, so that the net result remains ambiguous. Moreover, this type of argument applies more directly to internal protection than to national defense. With increasingly complex defense technology and the substitution of military hardware for (conscripted or underpaid) military manpower, it is not surprising to find a rising trend in the ratio of defense expenditure to GNP. A less direct contribution of war finance to public sector growth has been its effect on the trend of civilian expenditures. By raising the threshold of what the public is willing to accept as a tolerable tax ratio, the temporary increase in the defense expenditure level during wars may have served as a wedge for subsequent expansion of civilian expenditures.

TRANSFERS

Considerations such as these are more difficult to apply to the transfer component of the expenditure total. Viewing transfer payments as means of vertical redistribution, one might argue that the gains from equalization tend to become less as average income increases. The propensity for voluntary giving as a form of donor's consumption falls as the income of the donee rises. Or, viewed somewhat differently, the slope of the marginal social income utility schedule may be taken to level off when moving along the income axis. Moreover, the distribution of factor earnings tends to become more equal as income rises, thus reducing the need for redistribution. While these considerations suggest a declining transfer share, there are also some opposite considerations. Thus, society may find itself in a better position to sustain the efficiency cost or deadweight loss which results in the process of redistribution, and the income elasticity of giving may exceed unity as related to the donor's income. Once more it is difficult to balance out these considerations, but the forces which make for a declining transfer ratio may well be stronger.

Conclusion. While these considerations do not permit one to derive a unique law of expenditure growth, they show that economic speculation may be applied to the subject. Based on the assumption of an "efficient" (in the sense of Pareto-optimal) pattern of development, it is not surprising to find that public purchases have risen with GNP and, going further, to note that some increase in the ratio of public purchases has occurred.

Having said this, it is necessary, of course, to introduce political considerations as a further explanatory factor. The political development of Western countries during this century has been marked by the rise of popular democracy, and a shift in political balance towards left of center. Gaining in momentum in the aftermath of the great depression and of World War II, the rise of the welfare state was heralded in the mid-forties by Beveridge's *Full Employment in a Free Society*, with fiscal policy the central instrument of social improvement. This is reflected dramatically in the rise of social welfare expenditures, (be it through the medium of social insurance or direct support), both in relation to GNP and as a share of total expenditures. While mostly in the form of rising transfers, this development also involved expansion of social services in kind. Combined with a corresponding increase in the overall level of taxation and the rising share of direct (and progressive) taxes, income equalization emerged as a major object of social policy, and the budget became its prime instrument of implementation.

Stated in the terms of my earlier analysis, there occurred a dramatic change in the pattern of effective demand for budgetary provision, be it because of changing social attitudes, or because of a broadening distribution of fiscal power. Viewed less positively, the rising level of public services would be traced in part to defects in the political process of fiscal decisionmaking. Thus public services may be over-expanded because voters overestimate benefits relative to their own cost share, or because "bureaucrats" tend to maximize their budgets. Moreover, and this seems most important to me, public services may be voted as a second best (but politically more feasible) means of achieving redistributional objectives. Finally, it is difficult to say to what extent political attitudes towards redistribution changed (on the donors' side) because of genuine changes in social attitude or because growing political pressures from the left made this the lesser price to pay. Notwithstanding the mix of underlying causes, this development in my view has strengthened Western democracy and has contributed to rather than threatened the survival of decentralized market economy. This is in contrast to Marx' vision (in the Communist Manifesto) of progressive income taxation as a means of destroying capitalism. Far from it. Fiscal reform, as I see it, has been the prime instrument of gradual change to a more social form of democracy, and with this a major factor of strength in the Western world.

3.   *Economic Implications*

At the same time, the growth of the public sector is not without potentially detrimental effects on the functioning of the market economy; and such effects may become increasingly severe as the share of the public sector continues to expand.

EFFECTS ON WORK EFFORT

Disturbing effects on work incentives – or putting it more carefully, on the choice between goods and leisure – are more or less inevitable results of public sector growth. This difficulty could be avoided if taxes were imposed in lump sum fashion, i.e. such as to set liabilities independent of economic activity. In this case, taxes would leave the wage rate unaffected and there would be no disturbing effects on the choice between work and leisure. Such a revenue system would involve no efficiency cost, but it would be unacceptable on equity grounds. The very movement towards the more egalitarian society which spearheaded the public sector expansion of the last fifty years could not be disregardful of equity in taxation.

In fact, an increasing share of revenue came to be derived from taxes on income. Such taxes enter as a direct wedge between the gross and net price of labor services. By reducing the net wage rate, the taxpayer is induced to substitute leisure for income, i.e. to work less. At the same time, the tax leaves the taxpayer worse off, thus generating an income effect which tends to make him work more. There is no *a priori* basis for concluding which effect will dominate. However, it can be concluded that work effort will tend to be lower under a progressive rate structure than under a proportional one. Such is the case because the adverse substitution effect is a function of the higher (marginal) or bracket rate of tax, whereas the favorable income effect is a function of the lower average rate only.

Of course, not the entire revenue is derived from income taxation. Indirect taxes of various sorts (excises, sales and value added) still yield one half or more of the typical revenue total. Such taxes do not reduce the net wage rate in nominal terms, but they lower its real value by raising prices. Income and substitution effects again come into play, but the latter are now less prominent than under the income tax. This may be expected to be the case since such taxes tend to be regressive.

In short, it is evident that the potential effect of the tax structure on the income-leisure choice (effect on work effort) depends greatly on which type of taxes are used. Moreover, the expenditure side of budget policy also enters. Do not transfer payments return income to the private sector, thereby offsetting the effects of revenue collection? Such would be the case, if the formula by which transfers are granted was the same as that by which taxes are withdrawn, but such is not the case. Transfers are not made in the form of wage subsidies, but typically decline as earnings rise. The substitution effect of such transfers is similar to that resulting from a tax on earnings, and it is combined in this case with an income effect which further reduces work effort. In all, the detrimental substitution effect on lower incomes which results from redistributive transfers may well be more significant than that which is induced by progressive taxation at the upper end of the scale.

Turning now from transfers to public services, suppose first that such services are a substitute for privately purchased goods. In this case, since I can obtain publicly provided goods free of charge, there will be less need to surrender leisure in order to purchase private supplies. Ironically this effect will be the greater the more useful public services are in substituting for private purchases. It is also possible, however, for public services to be complementary to private consumption. Public broadcasting, for instance, will induce consumers to purchase recreation equipment. In this case, such services raise the value of income and exert a favorable substitution effect. Still another possibility is for public services to be complementary to private leisure, thus strengthening unfavorable effects on work incentives.

In all, it is evident that the effects of public sector expansion on work incentives can take various forms and it is not obvious what the net effect will be. Since there is no clear answer on theoretical grounds, the matter has to be resolved on an empirical basis. Certainly, the growth of the public sector has coincided as a matter of historical development with the growth of leisure time. The work week, in the course of the century, has declined by a third or more, vacation periods have lengthened greatly, the retirement age has been reduced and the intensity of effort (per hour of work) may well have declined. All this may reflect a high income elasticity of demand for leisure, decline in "work ethics" if you will. Or, it may have been a response to progressive taxation and of transfers in the course of public sector expansion. There is no ready way of distinguishing between these explanations. However, I find it difficult to escape the conclusion that continuing public sector expansion – especially if in the form of progressive taxation, equalizing transfers and public services which are complementary to leisure rather than to work – will, sooner or later, involve serious efficiency costs. Such at least would be the case unless other than market-based incentives could be strengthened.

24

Disturbing effects on resource allocation are not limited to the choice between work and leisure. Production and sales taxes on commodities enter as a wedge between gross and net prices, be it of commodities or factors of production. They therefore enter into consumer choices between products, or into producer choices between factor inputs. Thus a tax imposed on product x but not on y will raise the relative price of x, leading the consumer to substitute purchases of y for x. As a result, efficient choice between commodities is interfered with and the taxpayer's loss will exceed the gain (or revenue) which the Treasury derives. Subject to some qualifications to be noted later, general taxes tend to be less burdensome in this respect than selective ones, so that polity is well advised to rely on the former.

Similar considerations apply to differential taxation of capital income. Thus a profits tax applicable in the corporate sector only will cause capital to move from the taxed to tax free sectors, thereby causing inefficient capital allocation. This distortion is avoided if the tax applies to investment income in all industries. Similarly, preferential income tax treatment of certain forms of income such as capital gains tends to direct capital into forms in which income can be realized in this fashion; preferential treatment of home ownership results in excessive investment in residential housing and so forth.

These and other non-neutralities in the tax structure cause resource use to depart from its efficient pattern, thereby imposing a welfare loss or excess burden on the economy. In theory, such inefficiencies (as distinct from interference with the leisure-income choice) *can* be overcome by improved fiscal design, and therefore need not be an inherent barrier to public sector growth. In practice, the additional burden or surcharge may well grow as a percent of revenue as the public sector expands. Not only do marginal tax rates rise in the process, but pressures for special treatment and tax privileges expand with the overall level of taxation.

ECONOMIC GROWTH

I now turn to the effects of public sector expansion on economic growth. Viewed over the longer run, it is evident that this century has been one of rapid economic growth in the Western world, a process which has occurred along with the growth of the public sector. This holds not only for the first half of the century but also for the period from 1950 to 1975 when public sector expansion proceeded at the most rapid rate. The more recent record for selected countries is shown in Table 4, based on OECD data for 1960-71. With the resulting pattern depending greatly on what countries are included

Table 4

GDP GROWTH AND THE PUBLIC SECTOR*

	Num-ber	Average Annual Growth Rate 1960-71		As Percent of GDP (1971)	
		Per Capita GDP	Gross Fixed Capital Formation	Current Receipts	Current Expenditures
Canada	1	3.5	5.0	36	20
U.S.A.	2	2.6	3.9	30	21
Japan	3	2.5	14.3	22	9
Australia	4	3.0	5.4	23	13
Austria	5	4.3	6.6	37	15
Belgium	6	4.3	4.7	35	14
Denmark	7	4.1	7.0	45	22
Finland	8	4.5	3.9	38	17
France	9	4.6	3.5	38	12
Germany	10	3.8	5.5	38	17
Greece	11	7.0	8.0	27	13
Iceland	12	3.4	6.2	33	10
Ireland	13	3.7	9.8	34	15
Italy	14	4.5	4.0	34	14
Luxembourg	15	2.4	3.4	36	19
Netherlands	16	4.0	6.3	41	16
Norway	17	4.2	5.7	47	18
Portugal	18	6.3	6.0	24	15
Spain	19	6.1	3.0	23	11
Sweden	20	3.3	4.4	43	23
Switzerland	21	2.7	5.8	27	12
United Kingdom	22	2.1	4.2	37	18

* Based on *National Accounts for OECD Countries, 1960-71.*
  Where data for 1971 not available, 1970 is used.

or omitted, the scatters of Charts 1-3 are more instructive than regression coefficients. We find no clear relation between the level of taxation and economic growth (Chart 1) but some degree of negative relationship between

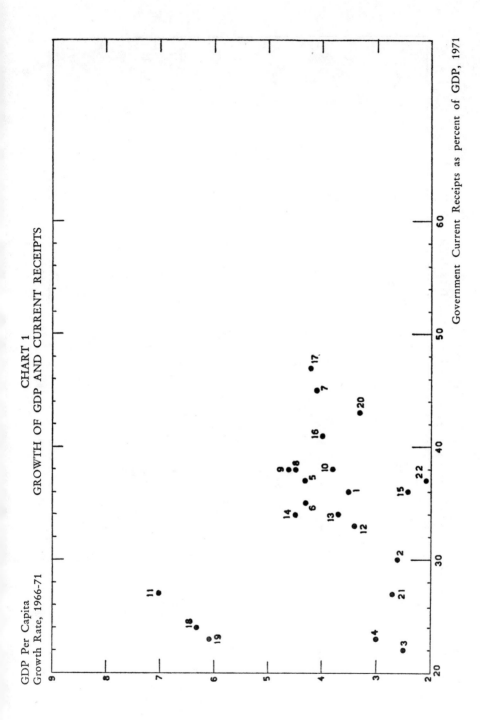

CHART 1
GROWTH OF GDP AND CURRENT RECEIPTS

GDP Per Capita
Growth Rate, 1966-71

Government Current Receipts as percent of GDP, 1971

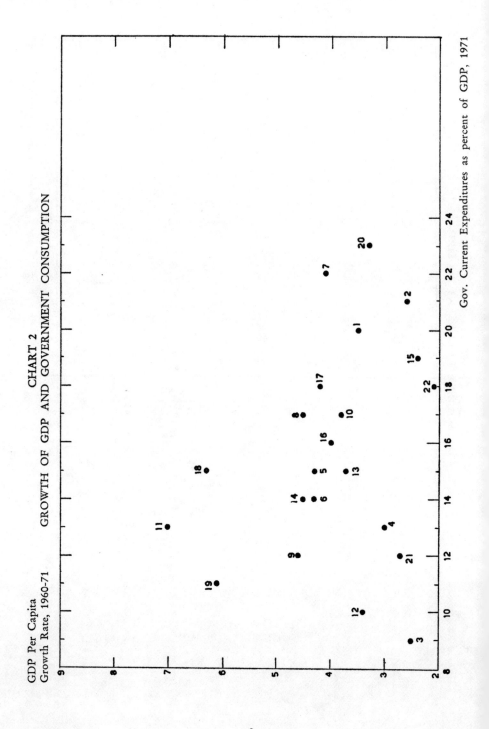

CHART 2

GROWTH OF GDP AND GOVERNMENT CONSUMPTION

GDP Per Capita
Growth Rate, 1960-71

Gov. Current Expenditures as percent of GDP, 1971

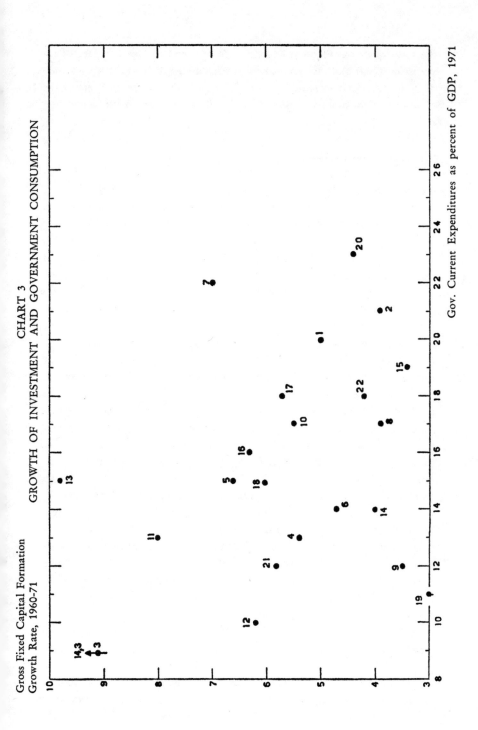

Gross Fixed Capital Formation
Growth Rate, 1960-71

CHART 3
GROWTH OF INVESTMENT AND GOVERNMENT CONSUMPTION

Gov. Current Expenditures as percent of GDP, 1971

the ratio of government consumption to GNP and the growth rate of investment (Chart 2). Since investment is related positively to the growth rate of GNP, the latter also stands in negative relation to the growth rate of the government consumption ratio (Chart 3). The relationship is not a strong one especially if the comparison is limited to West-European countries, but the data give some support to it. The stronger negative relationship with government consumption than with the tax rate suggests that the problem is not so much one of disincentive effects of taxation but of withdrawal of potentially investable resources from the private sector.[2]

Proceeding on the assumption of a neo-classical macro model, the *ex ante* savings which are intended to be made by the private sector will in fact find investment outlets. In such a setting public sector growth will affect the growth of the economy only through its effects on the rate of savings. Investment will take care of itself. Assuming tax finance, the question is whether the marginal propensity to save of the public sector (i.e. government saving out of tax revenue) falls short of, equals or exceeds that of the taxpayers. The answer depends on which taxes are used. The corporation profits tax reduces private savings more per dollar of revenue than most other taxes. The individual income tax tends to reduce private saving more (especially if progressive) than do consumption taxes and so forth. Moreover, the answer depends on how the government spends its proceeds. Typically, current expenditures of government exceed, rather than fall short of, current revenue, suggesting dissavings in the public sector. But much depends on how "current expenditures" are defined, i.e., on how the line between current and capital expenditures is drawn. Defining capital expenditures as acquisition of assets, as is done in the UN and OECD income accounts, the public sector savings rate is substantially below what it would be if various forms of human investment (e.g. teachers' or nurses' salaries) were included.

It is difficult, moreover, to compare recorded public sector savings rates with those in the private sector because the initial assumption of macro economic behavior which underlies this model – that *ex ante* savings in the private sector will always be invested – is unrealistic. The private sector may not operate so as to maintain full employment in an automatic fashion. This being the case, public dissaving (budget deficits or lesser rates of surplus) may be needed to provide an offset to potential excess *(ex ante)* saving in the private sector. However this may be, there is no need for public sector expansion to result in a shortage of saving. In theory at least, it should always be possible by creating a surplus to adjust fiscal policy so as to provide the desired overall (public plus private) rate of saving in the economy. Such public saving in turn need not be channeled into public capital formation, but may be made available to the private capital market through public lending. In short, monetary and fiscal policies can be combined in such a way as to secure the desired overall rate of saving.

Such at least is the case in the neo-classical model where investment automatically adjusts to saving. But such may not be the case, and the level of investment may be more difficult to control. Profit taxation is generally taken to reduce the net rate of return on investment, a detrimental effect which countries attempt to cushion through various forms of investment incentives. Moreover, allowance for loss offset reduces probable losses, just as the tax itself reduces probable gains. There is no need therefore for public sector expansion to be detrimental to investment in the private sector, but once more much depends on how the tax structure is designed. Since investment income accrues largely to the upper income groups, there tends to be a conflict between redistributional objectives and the desire to avoid detrimental effects on investment.

STABILIZATION

Finally a word need be said about the implications of public sector growth for economic stabilization, i.e. employment and inflation. Here it might be useful to distinguish between (1) the size of the public sector share and (2) its growth.

Regarding the former, there is good reason to expect that a large public sector will strengthen the built-in stability of the economy. Public expenditures are not subject to cyclical fluctuations as is private investment, and fluctuation in tax revenue in response to changes in the tax base tend to provide a degree of built-in stability which is helpful in offsetting fluctuations in private sector activity. While the stagnation prognosis of the thirties and forties proved a false alarm, the increased public share since World War II has surely added a factor of strength to economic performance.

One must be less optimistic however with regard to the effect of public sector growth on inflation. Just as deficits or public dissaving are a constructive instrument of public policy in periods of unemployment, so is deficit finance a destabilizing factor when undertaken to expand the public sector by means of an inflation tax. To what extent world wide inflation over the last decade has been due to mistaken budget policy of this sort is a matter of debate. Clearly, a deficient level of tax finance during the late sixties was a factor in initiating inflation in the United States, although other causes (rising raw material prices and cost-push factors) became the primary source later on. Similarly, excessively easy fiscal policy has been a factor in generating inflation in the U.K., Italy and other countries. Thus, public sector expansion can be a cause of inflation. While it need not be so, if proper discipline in the financing of public expenditures is maintained, inflation is not unlikely to be a by-product of public sector expansion.

4. Conclusions and Prospects

Having explored the facts of public sector growth and some of its economic implications, what are the lessons to be drawn for the future course of events?

A little over a hundred years ago (in 1873 to be precise), Adolph Wagner first expounded his law of expanding state activity. He proposed that a combination of social, economic and political forces would combine to make for a secular growth of the public sector, pushing budgetary activity ahead faster than the growth in total output. "Financial stringency," so he thought, "may hamper the expansion of state activity – but in the long run the desire for development of a progressive people will always overcome these fiscal difficulties."[3] Few historical prognoses, it appears, have proven so correct. But others were less fortunate. Bastable, writing in 1903, held that "15 percent was probably the largest proportion of the income that under ordinary conditions could be taken for the state services;"[4] Sir Josiah Stamp, writing in 1922, took a more flexible view, setting taxable capacity equal to what remains after adequate levels of private consumption and savings are provided for.[5] Colin Clark, finally, writing in 1945, laid down the thesis that taxation must not reach more than a quarter of a nation's income.[6] Currently, 49 percent would seem the highest imaginable level, and so it goes.

Given this array of false predictions, caution is in order. Nevertheless, it seems likely that expansion of the public sector share will proceed at a decreasing rate. In support of this is the simple fact (already noted by Wicksell) that the further the process of equalization proceeds, i.e., the further progressive taxation has advanced in capturing income from the top down, the lower comes to be the income class by which a further increase in the tax share must be borne. With this, the smaller will become the fraction of voters who will stand to be benefitted thereby. Moreover, as the general level of income rises, and with it the standards of living at the lower end of the scale, there may also be less pressure for further redistributive action. Both these considerations suggest that public sector expansion based on domestic redistribution will taper off. Moreover, as the level of taxation relative to GNP rises, so do the difficulties of avoiding excess burden or efficiency costs. Pointing in the other direction may be increasing concern with redistribution at the international level, a point to be dealt with in the next lecture. The implication of declining rates of population growth are ambiguous, since they will reduce the need for educational services while increasing that for old-age provision. Still other and less predictable factors will include changing defense costs or new public service needs which will result from technological change. Pending such developments, however, I would expect the recently fast rate of expansion in the public sector share to come to an at least temporary halt. Whether this is an optimistic or a pessimistic note on which to conclude this lecture, I shall leave to you to judge.

1 / A comparison of the price indices for GNP and government expenditures in the United Kingdom, as presented by Peacock and Wiseman for the years from 1890 to 1950, for instance, shows only a negligible divergence. See Alan T. Peacock and Jack Wiseman, *The Growth of Public Expenditure in the United Kingdom*, Princeton University Press, 1961, p. 155.

2 / See also David Smith, "Public Consumption and Economic Performance", *National Westminster Bank Quarterly Review*, November 1975.

3 / Adolph Wagner, *Finanzwissenschaft*, 1890, 3d edition, Part 1, p. 76.

4 / C.F. Bastable, *Public Finance*, 3d edition, McMillan, London 1903, p. 676.

5 / Sir Josiah Stamp, *Wealth and Taxable Capacity*, London, P.S. King, 1922, Ch. 4.

6 / Colin Clark, "Public Finance and Changes in the Value of Money", *Economic Journal*, LV (December 1945), p. 371.

SECOND LECTURE

Fiscal Redistribution

The driving force of public sector expansion, as noted in my first lecture, has been that of redistribution. Much of this was accounted for by explicit redistribution programs, be it through transfers or through low-income oriented expenditures in kind. Beyond this, expansion of general public services financed by progressive taxation contributed to the redistributive process. Moreover, fiscal redistribution has operated not only between individuals. Most countries also experienced a substantial increase in the flow of transfers between jurisdictions or levels of government; and, though not yet of major significance, there is the future prospect of increased concern with redistribution at the international level.

I.   *Distribution Among Persons*

Interpersonal distribution, and adjustments therein (i.e. redistribution), is a major concern of fiscal policy. How does it fit into the body of fiscal theory, how can it be measured and what has it accomplished?

THE CONCEPTUAL FRAMEWORK

To begin with, how does distribution policy fit into the framework of fiscal theory? When I developed my approach to this problem in the fifties, I thought it useful to distinguish between three major aspects of the fiscal function, i.e. the provision of social goods, redistribution and stabilization. I thought of these as performed by three branches of the budget, i.e. the allocation, distribution and stabilization branches. Each branch would prepare its budget while taking the policies of the other two as given, though the action of each would be co-determined with that of the others in a general equilibrium system. The transactions of the three budgets would then be netted out, and only the net budget would be implemented by taxes, transfers and purchase policies.[1] The purpose of this three-branch model was not to provide a description of actual budget policy. Rather, it was a heuristic device to distinguish between major policy objectives and to permit them to be pursued without interference with each other. Thereby, efficient budget policy would avoid the distortions which result if any one function is used not for its own purpose but to advance the objectives of another. Such distortions have played a major role in the historical process of fiscal development and they continue to do so. The model thus retains considerable merit as a framework for policy thinking, although conceptual separation of the allocation and distribution aspects of budget policy has run into certain objections which should be noted.

1. Since the basic issue of distribution is one of economic welfare, and hence of the distribution of goods, what is to be gained by introducing the distribution of money income in the first place? Indeed, the basic model of welfare economics, and Samuelson's inclusion of social goods therein, bypasses the issue of *money income* distribution altogether. It proceeds directly to the distribution of welfare. The first step is to determine the utility frontier, giving the efficient mix of private and social goods and distribution of the former, corresponding to all conceivable states of welfare distribution. The second step is to choose the optimal distribution of welfare as derived from a given social welfare function. Thus the basic objective of distribution policy as defined in terms of welfare may be dealt with directly, and nothing is gained by dealing with the distribution of income as a point of departure. This reasoning is compelling if we accept the assumptions, implicit in this procedure, (1) that there exists an omniscient referee who knows individual utility functions and can determine efficient allocations accordingly and (2) that the problem is one of assigning outputs among individuals, thereby setting an initial state of distribution. Both assumptions are useful in defining optimality, but they are of little help in dealing with a real-world fiscal process. Here preferences are not known and a given state of distribution already exists. Since preferences are unknown, preference revelation must be induced in order to permit efficient allocation. With regard to private goods this may be done through the play of effective demand in the market, while for social goods it must be done via a voting process. Either mechanism has to be based on a distribution of income, so that efficient allocation may be determined in relation to the latter. Moreover, the distribution issue must be dealt with not in *de novo* terms, but in a setting where a given state of distribution already exists, thus making the problem one of redistribution rather than of primary distribution.

For both reasons, the distribution of income must enter the model. At the same time, this poses an apparent difficulty. As was noted already by Wicksell, the resulting allocation can be optimal only if the underlying distribution of income may be considered optimal as well. Since this optimal distribution of income must be derived from the optimal distribution of welfare to which it is to give rise, it must be determined in relation to a particular pricing rule. This is the case because a person's welfare depends not only on the income which he receives but also on the prices which he must pay. Does this leave us in a position of circular reasoning, where relative prices are determined in line with a given income distribution, but determining the correct distribution of income involves knowledge of the relative prices that must be paid? The answer is no, because determination of the pricing rule introduces an additional equation into the model.[2] In the context of private goods the competitive solution of marginal cost pricing may be used as a convenient (and efficient) device as it permits reliance on market forces. In the social goods case, determination of the best pricing rule (i.e. the choice among various efficient rules) involves designing a voting process which – by linking tax and expenditure decisions – induces preference revelation with a minimum of "cheating". Viewed this way, separation of allocation and income distribution issues is not redundant. Far from it. It becomes an essential step, as I see it, in the formulation of a normative theory which provides a bridge to economic practice. This holds even for a world with private goods only, but the more so if social goods are added to the picture. Taxes (which do not appear in the pure allocation model of social goods theory) are needed not only to introduce preference revelation but also to transfer resources from the private to the public sector.

2. If the problem of distribution policy could be formulated in terms of assigning shares in a given stock of goods, it could be viewed as essentially an issue in social philosophy. Assignment or reassignment could then be handled through a process of lump sum taxes and transfers. But the actual problem is more complex, since it deals with the assignment of benefits generated by a continuing process of economic activity. Redistribution policy – be it on the taking or receiving end of the line – will thus affect the very process of economic activity. Lump sum taxes or transfers, at best, can be an instrument of once-and-for-all redistribution only. They cannot be used in a continuing fashion, since taxes and transfers must then be related to current earnings and other economic characteristics. Thus economic choices are disturbed and efficiency costs result. The problem then becomes one of introducing distributional corrections so as to minimize efficiency costs and of weighing the gains from redistribution against the efficiency losses that result.

This raises the question whether the tax-transfer process (i.e., the mechanism of a positive-negative income tax) provides the best instrument, as was implied in my interpretation of the distribution branch. The difficulty which arises is that the income tax-transfer process may interfere with the choice between (1) present and future consumption and (2) goods and leisure. This being the case there may be other types of taxes and transfers which might be used to accomplish redistributive objectives but which involve a lesser efficiency cost. In particular, discrimination in favor of leisure may be reduced by the taxation of goods which are complementary to leisure and the subsidization of goods which are complementary to work. Considerations of this sort establish a link between allocation and distribution issues. They have been given much attention in the recent literature on optimal commodity taxation, but their practical application is as yet to be explored. In the meantime chances are that efficiency considerations will be served best by relying on the income tax-transfer mechanism, rather than on a selective tax-subsidy process.

3. In recent years, attention has been focussed on redistribution as a voluntary process. If B's utility appears as an argument in A's utility function, A will make gifts to B as part of his own utility maximization. This approach leads to a concept of Pareto optimal redistribution, thus breaking the barrier which had come to be erected (in the so-called "new" welfare economics) between welfare economics and distributional considerations. Voluntary giving becomes part of the individual's budgeting process.[3]

This is a significant addition to the theoretical framework, but I would note two limitations. First, the scope of Pareto optimal redistribution is conditioned by the initial (or pre-gift) state of distribution. As such it covers only a secondary aspect of the distribution issue, while omitting what may be called the problem of primary distribution. Unless one assumes a Lockean rule of entitlement to the fruits of one's labor, the ethical issue of just distribution remains to be resolved. Moreover, the state of distribution may be viewed as a social good. Though an individual may be prepared to contribute to the welfare of others, his capacity to affect the overall pattern is so small as to make little difference. Hence, his willingness to participate may be contingent on that of others to do so as well, thus calling for a mandatory redistribution policy which is decided upon by vote and filtered through the budget process.

4. Finally, there is the fact that people's willingness to engage in redistribution (singly or subject to participation by others) may be conditional on the recipient using his transfer in an approved way. That is to say, giving may take the paternalistic form of giving in kind. The political process may be willing to support low income housing or food programs,

40

while it might not be willing (or less so) to support cash grants. This undoubtedly explains the extent to which redistributional policies have taken an in-kind form. This view, which has been referred to as "categorical equity" combines my concept of "merit goods" with that of distributive justice; it once more introduces a link between distributive considerations and the use of resources, but it does so in a way compatible with their separation in the context of the allocation branch.

5. Finally, there is the question of how the shape of optimal distribution is to be determined. From the thirties until recently, fiscal theorists have argued that the economist can say but little about the problem, the issue being one of social ethics (viewed normatively) or of fiscal politics (seen empirically). The concept of the social welfare function itself is only a reflection of underlying ethical criteria or political processes. A somewhat more positive view is taken by the recent literature on optimal income taxation. This literature attempts to determine an optimal rate structure under the income tax, while allowing for the responses of payers and payees, and thereby for the efficiency cost which the transfer involves. But the optimal rate structure thus arrived at still depends on the shape of the social welfare function that is postulated to begin with. It does not help us to determine what constitutes an equitable distribution, but only offers an improved way of dealing with the implementation of a given norm.

MEASUREMENT PROBLEMS

Leaving these theoretical issues, I now turn to the extent to which inter-individual redistribution has in fact been implemented. The difficulties involved in measuring the redistributive effort of the fiscal system are substantial. Let me divide them into the following questions:

(1) What is the base to which fiscal net benefits should be related?

(2) How is the distribution of tax burdens to be measured?

(3) How is the distribution of expenditure benefits to be measured?

(4) How severely are the results affected by failing to consider changes in pre-tax earnings?

(5) How are the results to be qualified if long run effects on capital formation and growth are to be allowed for?

Obviously, this is an imposing list of issues and I can deal with them only in abbreviated form.

Choosing the Base. Measuring the fiscal effects of redistribution calls for specifying what is being compared with what. Thus, the comparison may be between (1) the state of distribution that exists with the prevailing fiscal system and (2) that which would exist in its absence. The difference for any particular household is the net fiscal benefit or net fiscal burden which results from the fiscal operation. It equals the gains which the household derives from transfer payments and public services, minus the burden which it incurs because taxes must be paid. Measured in absolute terms, these net burdens or benefits may be derived by deducting (1) from (2) or (2) from (1), but the direction of movement matters when the absolute amounts are expressed as a percentage of either the post- or pre-budget distribution.

In the first case, the denominator of the ratio equals earnings plus transfers plus benefits from public services minus taxes. In this case, the resulting pattern of effective rates (positive for net benefits and negative for net burdens) shows the losses and benefits which would result as the budget is withdrawn. In the second case, the denominator is defined as the pre-budget state of distribution, i.e., earnings excluding transfers. The resulting pattern of effective rates now measures the distribution of burdens or benefits that would result as the budget is introduced. The distinction is an important one because the magnitude of redistribution – as measured by, say, the resulting change in the Gini coefficient – will be substantially larger for the introduction than for the removal case. This is obvious if we look at the lower end of the income scale where net benefits may raise earnings by several hundred percent, while net benefits as a percent of earnings plus net benefits can at the most reach 100 percent. The impression that relatively little redistribution has occurred seems to reflect the tendency to look at the latter rather than the former formulation of the problem.

Measuring Tax Burden. In measuring the distribution of tax burdens certain assumptions regarding tax incidence have to be made. Thus, it is generally held that the individual income tax rests with the payee and that commodity taxes are passed on to the consumer. Views are divided regarding the corporation tax. The predominant academic view takes it to fall on capital income, although a minority view shared by myself takes it to be transmitted at least in part to consumers or workers. Usually, alternative assumptions are allowed for. While formerly viewed as falling on the use of housing, the incidence of the property tax is now viewed largely as falling on capital income. Payroll taxes, finally, are usually imputed to the wage earner, especially so with regard to the employee contribution, and in most cases also with regard to the part contributed by the employer. Imputation of the entire tax to wage-earners is, of course, appropriate if one assumes a competitive labor market, but the actual operation of wage bargaining may be unaware of this rule.

Measuring Expenditure Benefits. Until fairly recently, focus in the distributional aspects of budget policy has been on the tax side only. But clearly the expenditure side must be included as well. This is easy with regard to transfer payments which, generally speaking, may be treated as negative taxes. Difficulties arise, however, with regard to public services. Here a distinction may be drawn between (1) effects on the pattern of factor earnings which result as public services are substituted for private purchases, and (2) the distribution of the benefits of public services. Regarding the latter, a further distinction may be drawn between (a) specific services the benefits of which may be attributed to particular groups of the population such as education, public health, highways and certain local services, and (b) services the benefits of which are more or less general and which cannot be imputed to particular groups of consumers.

As noted below, aspect (1) may be expected to be more or less neutral with regard to distribution, so that attention is focussed on aspect (2). Expenditures, the benefits of which permit selective imputation, typically account for the larger half of goods and service expenditures. Benefits from such expenditures may be attached to particular user groups – i.e. education may be imputed to school children or their parents, highway outlays may be assigned to users of highway facilities and so forth. In this fashion an approximate distribution of benefits may be obtained. There is a question of whether benefits received are measured properly in terms of expenditures made on behalf of various recipient groups or whether allowance should be made for differences in valuation. For instance, education as an investment may yield different returns to different student groups. Notwithstanding such differences, however, a general pattern of benefit distribution, defined in terms of expenditures "made on behalf of" various groups, offers a useful point of departure.

At the same time, there is no simple solution for benefits which are derived from general expenditures. If such benefits are available equally to all, as the pure theory of social goods suggests, benefits may be imputed on a per capita basis, i.e. be distributed equally (similar to a head tax) across income groups. It has been noted, however, that the resulting benefits, while similar in physical terms, should be valued more highly for upper-income recipients. If "sold" under a rule of benefit taxation, such recipients would be willing to pay more.[4] Given such an adjustment, the equalizing effects of a per capita allocation would be voided, and the benefit distribution might become more nearly in line with a proportional pattern.

Given the difficulty of allocating general benefits, one might argue that they had best be excluded and some studies have proceeded on that basis. However, this introduces a new complication into the derivation of net benefits since it becomes difficult to decide which part of the tax revenue should be omitted on the other side of the equation. Given the impossibility of determining the "marginal" tax dollar, the easiest procedure is to assume that general expenditures are paid for by the average tax dollar, thus permitting a corresponding across-the-board cut in tax burdens.

Further difficulties. Two further difficulties need be noted, difficulties which apply to both the tax and expenditure sides of the equation. Both relate to the fact that the estimating procedure does not allow for a genuinely general equilibrium analysis. To begin with, the procedure just described takes the distribution of earnings as a point of departure and then deducts estimated tax burdens and adds estimated benefits for the case of budget introduction, or vice versa, for the case of budget removal. The question is whether it can in fact be assumed that the underlying distribution of earnings remains unchanged. Surely, removal or introduction of the budget will produce changes in factor earnings and factor prices which in turn will affect relative income positions, changes which will have to be allowed for in addition to those recorded directly by the imputation of tax burdens or expenditure benefits. Such changes will indeed occur. The relative position of particular households will be changed, but one need not expect this to result in systematic changes in the size distribution of income. I base this on the hypothesis (1) that earnings which originate in output produced in response to government demand, be it in public employment or in purchases from the private sector, are distributed in about the same pattern as are earnings generated in meeting private sector demands; and (2) that there is only a random relationship between the pattern in which the consumption of particular products is distributed among high and low income households, and the way in which earnings generated in the production of these products are distributed among income groups. Thus, I see no strong reason to believe that the assumption of a constant earnings distribution will introduce a systematic bias.

It may also be noted that we are dealing here with an analysis of net benefits or burdens, combining the effects due to both the tax and expenditure side. If the tax or expenditure sides are considered in isolation, the question arises how the resulting change in aggregate demand is to be accounted for. As a possible procedure, it may then be helpful to view the problem of burden or benefit incidence in differential terms, e.g., to compare the burden distribution under actual taxes with that which would result if a similar revenue were obtained from a proportional system. Once more, the need to allow for aggregate demand effects is reduced because the state of budgetary balance is held unchanged.

Failure to allow for long run effects may pose a more serious difficulty. A tax-transfer policy which in the short run benefits low income groups at the cost of high income groups may have long run effects which have a bearing, not only on the income position of high, but also on that of low income recipients. By reducing the rate of saving and growth, the future level of earnings may be depressed, including factor earnings at all levels of the income scale. Just how the pattern of distribution will be affected will depend on the production function and the resulting changes (or absence thereof) in factor shares. Assuming shares to remain more or less unchanged (as most empirical analysis seems to suggest) there will be no major effects on distribution, with a lower level of income (or a lesser increase) being shared throughout. All this adds to the complexities of the problem and makes it necessary to distinguish between measuring incidence in terms of (1) net rates of return on various factors, and (2) the income shares received by various income groups. The shape of distribution between generations is added to that between individuals or households, thereby increasing the complexity of the problem.

NET EFFECTS

Having surveyed some of the difficulties of measuring fiscal redistribution I now turn to the findings. I begin with the picture of the United States, with which I am most familiar, and then proceed to a brief comparison with some other countries.

U.S. Pattern. The importance of fiscal redistribution in the United States may be assessed best by comparing various distributive patterns, including (1) the distribution of earnings, (2) the distribution of earnings plus transfers or income as usually defined and (3) the distribution of income available for private use, or earnings plus transfers minus taxes. As will be seen in Table 5, these distributions become increasingly equal, with the lowest quartile receiving 4.5, 8.5 and 9.5 respectively, while the share of the highest quartile declines from 51 to 48 and 46 percent. If benefits from specific public services are included, the lowest quartile share rises to over 10 percent. If general benefits are included on a per capita basis (see line 5), it would come to exceed 15 percent, with the top quartile share falling to 40 percent. Including general benefits on a proportional to income basis (line 6), redistribution is less but the corresponding ratios are still 13 and 44 percent. Whether one wishes to consider these outcomes as too little or too much may be a matter of social value. But compared to the much lesser change in the distribution of earnings, as may be observed over decades, it seems to me that the results are quite substantial. Moreover, given a social

Table 5

	Lowest Quartile	Second Quartile	Third Quartile	Highest Quartile	Total
Income Distribution					
1. Earnings	4.5	17.2	26.7	51.1	100
2. Earnings plus transfers	8.5	17.5	25.5	48.5	100
3. Disposable Income	9.9	18.7	25.2	45.7	100
4. Total, Post Budget, excluding Gen. Benefits	10.1	17.9	24.7	46.5	100
5. Total, Post Budget, including Gen. Benefits (a)	15.6	19.7	24.4	40.1	100
6. Total, Post Budget, including Gen. Benefits (b)	13.1	18.5	24.5	43.9	100
As % of Income (line 2)					
7. Taxes	23.9	29.4	36.2	38.4	35.0
8. Transfers	43.8	8.3	3.2	1.5	7.1
9. Specific benefits	13.5	10.4	8.5	7.0	11.4
10. General Benefits (a)	49.2	23.9	16.3	8.6	16.7
11. General Benefits (b)	9.0	15.0	16.3	18.9	16.7
12. Net Benefits (a)	117.1	13.2	—8.2	—21.0	—
13. Net Benefits (b)	76.9	3.3	—8.2	—10.7	—
14. Net Benefits excluding Gen. Benefits	29.3	3.5	—7.1	—15.4	—
As % of Earnings (line 7)					
15. Net Benefits (a)	216.3	14.4	—8.5	—21.4	—
16. Net Benefits excluding Gen. Benefits	146.5	3.8	—7.3	—11.4	—
As % of Post Budget Total Income					
17. Net Benefits (12/5)	53.9	16.8	—12.4	—13.9	—
18. Net Benefits excluding Gen. Benefits (14/4)	99.2	14.0	—9.2	—9.5	—

* Footnotes, see p. 47.

welfare function which values gains at the bottom of the scale more heavily than losses at the top, the degree of redistribution which is being accomplished must surely be considered of significant magnitude.[5] In any case, these results do not seem to support the view frequently heard, that efforts at redistribution involve a great deal of churning without leading to a significant change in the prevailing pattern.

The elements entering into this outcome, as shown in the lower part of Table 5, are a tax burden distribution which is slightly progressive below and about proportional above the midpoint of the income scale (line 7), a transfer distribution which shows a very high ratio of transfers to earnings at the lower quartile while declining rapidly thereafter (line 8), and a distribution of allocable specific expenditure benefits which is mildly pro-low income (line 9). The dominant factor in the picture is clearly the highly pro-low distribution of transfer payments. As shown in the table, net benefits (line 12 and 13) reach their break-even point at about the middle of the income scale. It may also be noted that the net benefit ratio at the lower end of the scale is substantially larger if related to earnings (line 15) than if related to income including transfers (line 12), whereas the ratios are more or less similar for the upper end of the scale. The ratios are reduced further, especially at the lower end of the scale, if related to income defined so as to include all expenditure benefits (line 17). As noted above, redistribution is more impressive if viewed in terms of budget introduction (line 12) than in terms of budget removal (line 17).

Other Countries. A more or less similar pattern may be found in other countries. While results vary somewhat due to differences in both contents and levels of budget operation, we find throughout, that the major agent of redistribution is on the transfer rather than on the tax side of the budget system. Even for countries which have substantially higher marginal rates of income tax than does the United States, the redistributive contribution from the tax side is modest relative to that from the expenditure and especially transfer side. Thus, in the U.K., it is estimated that fiscal equalization in 1971 resulted in a reduction in the Gini coefficient from 34.0 to

* See R.A. Musgrave, Karl E. Case and Herman Leonard, "The Distribution of Fiscal Burdens and Benefits", *Public Finance Quarterly*, June 1974.
  Lines 10-17: (a) involves benefit allocation on per capita basis; (b) on proportion to income basis.
  Line 17: Total post budget income used as denominator equals earnings plus transfers plus special expenditure benefits plus general expenditure benefits minus taxes.
  Line 18: In determining the denominator, taxes are reduced by a fraction equal to the share of general benefits in total benefits.

25.0, i.e., in a shift towards equality by 26 percent. To this, expenditure benefits (limited in this study to transfers and direct subsidies) contributed 8.1 percentage points, direct taxes contributed 2.5 percentage points and indirect taxes —1.6 percentage points. Thus, the expenditure side accounted for above 90 percent of the total increase in equality.[6] For Sweden, with its relatively large public sector, we find once more that the redistributive expenditure effect far outweighs the tax side although in this case expenditures in kind are of greater importance than those of the transfer type.[7]

Conclusion. In all, it appears that fiscal redistribution has been substantial but that, contrary to traditional preoccupation with the progressivity of the tax structure, the cutting edge of redistribution has been on the expenditure side of the budget. Moreover, such redistribution as has occurred has been highly concentrated at the bottom end of the income scale, reflecting society's concern with relieving poverty rather than with an overall reduction of inequality as measured by a change in the overall Gini coefficient. For reasons noted in the preceding lecture, it may well be that this trend has reached a plateau, but its effect has been of significant magnitude, especially if viewed in terms of budget introduction rather than withdrawal. Before proceeding, one qualification should be added. This is to note that our analysis has been in terms of annual cross section data, rather than in terms of life-time incomes. This may be taken to overstate the degree of redistribution on both the transfer and tax side. Thus transfers are received during the low phases of the life-income cycle (especially in old age) or during temporary income lows, such as periods of unemployment. Similarly, high rates of progressive taxation are borne by normally lower income recipients during occasional high income years, and low rates are paid by normally high income recipients during a temporary low. Thus the pattern of life-time redistribution which, from some points of view, is the more relevant one would be less marked than that recorded on an annual income basis.

2. *Inter-Jurisdictional Redistribution*

We now turn from inter-individual to inter-jurisdictional transfers. These also have experienced rapid expansion. This at least is the case in countries (such as the USA, Canada, Australia, Switzerland or Germany) which traditionally have relied on a relatively decentralized fiscal system. In this fashion it has been possible to retain decentralization of expenditure decisions while permitting increased use of central revenue sources, such as the income tax, which are best administered at the national level. Where revenue from shared taxes is simply returned to the jurisdiction of origin, no interjurisdictional redistribution occurs. But most transfers are not of this sort. Rather, they are designed to shift fiscal resources between jurisdictions. What is the rationale for such interjurisdictional redistribution and how does it relate to redistribution among individuals?

The answer depends on one's interpretation of fiscal federalism. Among others, the following interpretations may be noted :

1. Transfers are made to narrow the gap between the average incomes of individuals in high and low income jurisdictions;
2. Transfers are made to equalize the conditions under which public services are provided in various jurisdictions, including (a) the tax price, (b) the payoff on tax effort, and (c) the effects of income or wealth differentials;
3. Transfers are made to assure individuals in all jurisdictions a certain minimum level of public service provision.

INCOME EQUALIZATION

The first approach is open to two interpretations. One is that the differences in average incomes within various jurisdictions are in themselves a matter of policy concern. The other is that transfer of fiscal resources from high to low income communities is a device for shifting income from high to low income individuals. Given the former and collective view, it makes no difference how the fiscal resources are raised in the paying and disbursed in the receiving unit. Under the latter or individualistic interpretation, it is important that transfers should flow from high income individuals to low income individuals, not merely from high average to low average jurisdictions. It follows that the logic of the former approach is compatible with transfer from jurisdiction H (with high average income) to jurisdiction L (with low average income), leaving it to H to decide on how the funds are to be raised and to L on how they are to be disbursed. But the logic of the second version calls for a tax-transfer system in which the income bases in H and L are joined, i.e. for a federal-type income-transfer scheme between persons. Only in this case will it be avoided that low income taxpayers in H may be called upon to contribute to high income taxpayers in L. The existing system in Federal countries typically falls between the two extremes. Whereas the transfer is financed on a Federation-wide basis, the disbursement pattern is left to the receiving jurisdiction.

A case for redistribution as a local fiscal function has been made in the context of the voluntary-giving approach, the argument being that donors

49

are more interested in the welfare of their neighbors than that of distant populations. This consideration has some merit in the absence of mobility, but once mobility is allowed for, interindividual redistribution must be largely a central function. This is the case because undertaken in sub-jurisdictions, it leads to a flight of tax bases (high income individuals and firms) out of the redistribution oriented jurisdictions, just as it leads to an inflow of potential beneficiaries. This, of course, has been a major factor in the fiscal difficulties which have arisen in urban centers in the United States. It is, it appears, also a factor of increasing importance in the common market and indeed on an international scale.

CONDITION-EQUALIZATION

The logic of income equalization does not call for constraints on the receiving jurisdiction as to how the transfer receipts are to be used. They may be used either for payments to the constituents (i.e. for tax reduction) or for the provision of various public services. Such is not the case if the very purpose of interjurisdictional transfers is to equalize the conditions under which public services may be provided. Once more, this objective may be interpreted in various ways.

Tax-Price Equalization. One rule may be to equalize the per capita cost or tax-price of providing public services. The per-capita cost of a unit of public services to an individual, depends on (1) the unit cost to the community, and (2) the number of taxpayers among whom this cost is shared. Assuming (1) to be the same for two communities, per capita costs will be less in the more populous jurisdiction and its equalization will call for transfers from the larger to the smaller unit. Such at least will be the case if we deal with the provision of pure social goods in which congestion costs are absent.

Equalization of Return to Effort. Another and quite different objective may be to equalize the tax effort (i.e. tax *rate*) required to provide a given level of public services. Among jurisdictions of equal service cost, this would call for transfers from high to low income jurisdictions. The mechanism, moreover, would take the form of taxes on and matching grants to public services, with the rates of tax related directly and those of grants related inversely to the level of income. In analogy to Pigouvian taxation theory, the rationale of this mechanism may be interpreted as a method of equalizing the sacrifice which has to be incurred in various jurisdictions to obtain a given level of public services. If the same tax rate provides equal services, it might be argued (under the assumption of unit elasticity of marginal income utility) that equal degrees of sacrifice lead to equal service levels.

Wealth Neutralization. As distinct from equalizing tax price or the return to tax effort, the transfer system may be designed to neutralize the effects of wealth or income differentials on the level of public services that is provided. This dependence has been noted in recent developments in the United States in the context of school finance. Since school expenditures are largely financed by local property taxes, and since the property tax base differs among communities, it has been held unfair for children in low-base communities to be deprived of adequate educational facilities. A remedy would be provided through a transfer system which neutralizes the effects of tax base differentials. This is not accomplished by equalizing the return to tax effort, but calls for a more complex transfer pattern.[8]

PERFORMANCE EQUALIZATION

Whereas the preceding three approaches are designed, in various ways, to equalize the conditions under which public services are provided by each jurisdiction, there was no attempt to equalize actual performance levels. Still another approach chooses the latter objective. In this case, the Federal grant aims at assuring minimum levels of provision for certain public services which, though provided in decentralized fashion by the member-jurisdictions, are to be enjoyed by all residents of the Federation. In this case matching grants are required, subject to a ceiling when the stipulated level of provision is reached. Such grants may have to be paid even to high income jurisdictions, where community preferences are such as to render inadequate provision at a non-subsidized price.

CONCLUSION

Among the various transfer patterns here surveyed, only the first (or income equalization) is of a purely redistributive nature; and this, as we have seen, calls for transfers in a unitary system rather than for an inter-jurisdictional transfer mechanism. Given sufficient time, it would be interesting to explore just how significant the various transfer objectives figure in the grant systems of various countries, and how they enter into present and future grant designs for the Common Market. However, I shall leave this aside so that, in the remaining minutes, a word may be said about the even broader problem of inter-national redistribution.

3. *Inter-Nation Redistribution*

It is not surprising, at second thought, that the inter-individual distribution of income on a world-wide basis is substantially more unequal than within nations. This is the case because there are sharp differences in mean incomes, with a large part of the world population living at a level of per-capita income about one-twentieth that of the highly developed countries. Moreover, income in low-income countries is frequently distributed less equally than in high income countries.

This vast income differential is well on its way to become an increasing source of international friction, the more so as the income gap between developing and developed countries tends to widen, rather than to narrow. Adjustments in trade policies and private capital flows may make some contribution to relieving the problem, but I doubt whether they can go very far in dealing with it. Chances are that a more direct approach will be demanded sooner or later and become the subject of discussion. Some rough estimates may be offered to gauge the magnitude of the problem.

Suppose for instance that it had been decided in 1975 to set a per capita floor of GNP at $ 200. If transfers had been made through a worldwide negative income tax (excluding China and the Soviet Union) to individuals with a lower income, I estimate that a total transfer budget of about $ 80 billion would have been required. Of this, $ 57 billion would have gone to India alone. Assuming finance (a) by a steeply progressive tax which lops off incomes from the top down, the contribution of U.S. residents would have been 18 percent of the total and the remaining ceiling income per capita would have been around $ 13,000. If the transfer had been financed (b) by a proportional tax on per capita income in excess of the floor, a rate of 2 percent would have been required, and the U.S. contribution would have risen to 35 percent. The U.S. contribution as percent of U.S. GDP would have been 1 and 2 percent respectively. If, instead, we were to postulate a per capita floor of $ 400, the required transfer budget would have risen to about $ 260 billion, and the U.S. contribution would have been 43 and 37 percent under the two financing methods respectively. The U.S. contribution as percent of GDP would now have been 8 and 6.9 percent. Most Western European countries would also have been in the contributing group, though at a lesser rate.[9]

These figures, I should note, do not include China and the Soviet Union. Inclusion of China might increase the transfer budget by 50 percent. Using the $ 200 ceiling, the U.S. contribution would rise to about 3 percent of GDP, while it would climb to about 10 percent if a $ 400 ceiling was set.

Inclusion of the Soviet Union (here left out due to lack of data) would add to the financing base under the proportional tax, though not under the progressive method. Whether such transfers will ever be considered and how far they will go remains to be seen. Other approaches in terms of trade or loan policy may prove more feasible and be tried first. Nevertheless, it is of interest to obtain an idea of the magnitudes that are involved. The results, of course, depend altogether on the income floor that is set. Note, moreover, that the amounts here estimated do not reflect a simple transfer from countries with high average incomes to those with low average incomes, but a genuine worldwide negative income tax, such that high income recipients in low income countries contribute while very low income recipients in high income countries may be on the receiving side. Such an arrangement, while more meaningful than inter-country transfers, also places greater demands on implementation through an international fiscal system.

In conclusion, it is evident that concern with distributional aspects of the fiscal function will continue to grow in importance, shifting in emphasis from a purely intra-jurisdictional to an inter-jurisdictional and eventually inter-national form. This development on the expenditure side will parallel other trends toward internationalization which, in the next lecture, we shall observe as well on the revenue side of budget policy.

1 / See my *Theory of Public Finance*, McGraw-Hill, 1958, Part 1.

2 / We have (1) the "correct" distribution of money income as a function of the "correct" distribution of welfare, and of a given set of relative prices, (2) the determination of prices on the basis of a given pricing rule, and (3) choice of the pricing rule such as to permit preference revelation through the market or the voting process.

3 / See H.H. Hochman and J.D. Rogers, "Pareto Optimal Redistribution", *American Economic Review*, September 1969.

4 / See H. Aaron and M. McGuire, "Public Goods and Income Distribution", *Econometrica*, vol. 38, pp. 907-918. It may be noted that a similar adjustment would be appropriate for services (though not transfers) which permit selective imputation.

5 / See A.B. Atkinson, "Poverty and Income Inequality in Britain", in *Poverty, Inequality and Class Structure*, Wedderburn (ed.), Cambridge University Press, 1974.

6 / See J.L. Nicholson, "The Distribution and Redistribution of Income in the United Kingdom," in *Poverty, Inequality and Class Structure*, Dorothy Wedderburn, ed.

7 / See Thomas Franzen, Kerstin Lörgren and Irma Rosenberg, "Redistributional Effects of Taxes and Public Expenditures in Sweden," *The Swedish Journal of Economics*, Vol. 7, 1975, No. 1.

8 / See Martin Feldstein, "Wealth Neutrality and Social Choice in Public Education," *AER*, March 1975.

9 / The calculations are based on a sample of over 70 developed and developing countries. The GNP figures are for 1975 and distribution estimates, based on World Bank sources for various years and countries are used. Details on data and procedure are available from the author. I am indebted to Peter Jarrett who has carried out the computation.

THIRD LECTURE

The Good Tax System

The literature on taxation may be divided into two parts – one which tells us what virtue the good tax structure ought to possess, and the other which deals with the vices which actual tax structures are found to exhibit. Thus the student of taxation suffers from a love-hate relationship to his subject and it is not easy to know which side one is on. This discussion, I hope, will make a modest contribution to the resolution of this conflict.

I. *Benefit vs. Ability Rule*

There are two great traditions in the theory of taxation, one is the ability to pay and the other the benefit strand. Both date back to Adam Smith and earlier. Both are contained in his first maxim "that the subjects of every State ought to contribute to the support of the government, as nearly as possible, in proportion to their respective abilities, that is in proportion to the revenue which they respectively enjoy under the protection of the State." There is some question whether Smith should be classified as a benefit or as an ability theorist but it is interesting to note that he included both in his maxim of equitable taxation. Subsequently, most of the effort, from John Stuart Mill on, came to be directed at the ability strand. The benefit approach for a long period was stifled by adherence to a protection theory of the state, but then reemerged in quite different form in the marginal utility analysis of the late 19th century. As formulated by Knut Wicksell and later on by Eric Lindahl, it proved an important forerunner of the modern theory of social goods.

The essence of the ability-to-pay approach is to ask this question: assuming that resources are to be withdrawn from the private sector, how should the burden be distributed in an equitable fashion? Moreover, the analysis can be extended to include transfer payments as negative taxes, thus covering the entire distribution function. After all, if the loss of private income due to the tax-finance of public service should be distributed in an equitable fashion, why should not the same consideration apply also to the total of remaining private income? If, in the Edgeworth-Pigou tradition, the cost of public services is to be distributed by the equal marginal sacrifice rule, why not distribute all income available for private use so as to maximize marginal utility or total welfare? Of course, this approach came under severe criticism as the new welfare economics from Robbins on made inter-personal utility comparisons unacceptable. But its spirit is still with us. It has been resurrected in recent years in "optimal tax" theory by specifying a social welfare function and maximizing welfare (or minimizing welfare loss) on that basis. However, in either case tax burdens are dealt with independent of the benefits received from public services, and this is the basic weakness of both the old and new formulation.

As I have noted in the last lecture, an operational theory of social goods cannot take preferences to be known and solve the problems of allocation and distribution in *de-novo* terms. The real-world setting is one in which there exists a given distribution of money income and in which taxes must be imposed to transfer recources to public use. Most important, consumer preferences are unknown. The crucial role of assigning tax prices in this setting (a term more appropriate than that of distributing tax "burdens") is to induce preference revelation by voting on tax-expenditure issues. This is essentially the spirit of benefit taxation. Ideally, the voting process would be one where all conceivable cost distributions (tax-prices payable by various individuals) would be matched with all conceivable public service programs, but this is hardly feasible. Selected expenditure and tax programs must be considered and tax programs must be expressed in terms of generally applicable tax formulae, rather than as a set of individual tax-prices.

Viewed in this way, the problem of designing a good tax system is to find that tax formula or set of tax formulae which will be most successful in securing preference revelation with a minimum of cheating. Such a tax is efficient in paving the way for optimal resource use. Moreover, it is equitable provided that the distribution of money income, as outlined in the second lecture, is determined with the particular tax formula or pricing rule for public services in mind. Whether this is to be the Lindahl price (the price which equals the consumer's marginal rate of substitution in consumption) is a different matter. While the Lindahl pricing rule is a prime contender, if only because of its analogy to private good pricing, it is not the only efficient rule that may be used.

Seen in the context of public goods provision, the design of the good tax structure must thus be undertaken in the spirit of benefit taxation, leaving the distribution problem to be dealt with in the ability-to-pay context. Whereas vertical equity in the ability framework is a matter of income utility or social welfare function, the problem of progression in the benefit context becomes one of income (and price) elasticity of demand for public services. But though the principle is clear, I must admit that it is difficult to determine which tax base (e.g. income or consumption) will be suited best to induce preference revelation. Perhaps a consumption or expenditure tax is suitable for the finance of public consumption, while a tax on saving is relevant for the finance of public capital formation.

2. *The Ability Base: Basic Issues*

Having raised these basic issues, let me now leave the realm of benefit taxation and proceed to consider in more detail the problem of tax base definition under the ability approach.

From J. S. Mill and Edgeworth to Pigou there has been a convention to discuss ability in terms of sacrifice and to define sacrifice in relation to income loss. Focus has been on the utility lost by surrendering successive amounts of income. These authors did not concern themselves much with how income should be defined for the purpose, but the problem of income definition has been dealt with at great length by continental (especially German) writers such as Schanz and it was developed further in the U.S. in the writings of Haig and Henry Simons. Indeed, a voluminous post-war literature has focussed on the proper definition of income.[1] However, this literature has not been concerned sufficiently with the prior question whether income is in fact the best point of departure for defining ability.

HORIZONTAL EQUITY

If the good tax system is to be one which distributes the burden in line with ability, the crucial problem is to define the index by which ability is to be measured. Given this index, the principle of horizontal equity requires that people with equal ability, or people in equal positions, should be treated equally. Putting it differently, people who are in equal position prior to tax should incur equal burdens and thus find themselves in equal positions after tax. But how is one to determine whether people are or remain in "equal" position?

Clearly, the indicator must relate to a person's economic capacity and not to other characteristics such as size, weight or date of birth. Moreover, the economic characteristics in terms of which equal position is defined must be sufficiently broad to include all aspects of economic capacity. This is the spirit in which the accretion concept of income was proposed as the most appropriate base, with accretion defined as addition to wealth from all sources, treated globally and independent of type of use. Alternatively, the base may be defined as the sum of consumption, accumulation and all other uses to which accretion may be put. But even this global concept of income use or income source is not a wholly satisfactory solution. One difficulty is that a person's tax burden will differ, depending on how he chooses to time his consumption. An income tax, by including interest income in the base, discriminates against the saver. This may be avoided by choosing consumption as the base. But with either base there remains the problem that a person's welfare not only includes his consumption and capacity to make transfers, but also his enjoyment of leisure. The leisure component of welfare (or economic capacity) remains tax-free under both the income or consumption approach.

The perfect formulation would consider people in equal positions – and subject to equal tax – if they are confronted with an equal set of options, and independent of the choice which they make among them. This would be accomplished by a tax on potential consumption, defined to include actual consumption, transfers and leisure, with all these measured on a present value base. Unfortunately, however, such a concept is not operational. For one thing, people's potential earning capacities differ and are not known. They may choose to work at a more pleasant but lower paying job than is available to them, so that the opportunity cost of leisure is not readily determined. For another, people's tastes differ, so that people with equal options may choose different consumption and leisure patterns. Equal positions, therefore, can no longer be taken to imply equal options and it no longer follows that people with equal options will be in equal positions. People in equal pre-tax positions with regard to income and to leisure, when subjected to the same tax formula, may incur different burdens and be left in different post-tax positions since they may suffer a different dead-weight loss or efficiency cost.

In view of all this, it appears that much of the tax-base discussion has been on a shaky foundation and that, given the fact of differing tastes, the problem may prove an intractable one. A second-best solution to the problem of tax base definition will have to suffice. This is unfortunate, but I do not consider it a cause for despair. The fact that a first-best solution is not available does not mean that a random choice will do as well as the second-best. As a general rule, it may be concluded that a broad definition, such as accretion for the income base or total consumption for the consumption base, is preferable to a narrow one such as income from barber shops or consumption of peanuts only.

As between the two broad bases, some case can be made that the equal option concept is served better by the consumption than the income base since it avoids placing a tax penalty on saving. At the same time, "consumption" should be defined to include not only "own-consumption" but also transfers by gifts and bequests, so that the base is broadened to cover all options of use.

This, of course, still leaves out leisure as a component of welfare, a serious defect on both equity and efficiency grounds. To overcome the dead-weight loss resulting from the substitution of leisure for income or consumption, the tax base may concentrate on products which have low elasticities of substitution or which are complementary to leisure. Such a restriction of the tax base, however, would at the same time interfere with considerations of horizontal equity. Since tastes differ, it would impose differential burdens on households which are initially in equal positions. It appears that, short of taxing potential income or consumption, there is no ready way in which consideration of equity and efficiency can be fully reconciled.

VERTICAL EQUITY

This much for the issue of tax base, as it relates to horizontal equity and efficiency considerations. The other question – no less difficult to resolve – is that of setting the pattern of differentiation in the treatment of people in unequal positions. This is the problem of vertical equity or rate structure. Here the approach has shifted from the Pigouvian formulation of interpersonal utility comparison, equal marginal utility schedules and specified sacrifice rules (equal absolute, proportional and marginal) to one of postulating a social welfare function. Social utilities are assigned to marginal income dollars and optimal tax rates (or transfer patterns) may be determined on that basis.[2] For certain social welfare functions, an ordinal comparison suffices while for others cardinal comparability in terms of socially valued utilities is needed.

The important contribution of this reformulation is to allow for the fact that the optimal tax-transfer system not only depends on the social welfare function but also on the utility functions of the individuals concerned. Individuals who are taxed will substitute leisure for income, and the resulting efficiency cost will be part of the welfare loss which they incur. This welfare loss must be weighed against the social gains from equalization, thus setting a limit to the appropriate degree of redistribution or progression. While the final answer still depends on the shape of the social welfare function (i.e. the community's judgment regarding the importance of equality) it is also conditioned by the responses which will result. Only in the extreme case (the Rawls maxi-min form of welfare function) will a zero weight be assigned to the losses which result above the break-even point, i.e. will redistribution be carried to the point at which no further increase in welfare at the bottom of the scale can be brought about. The problem of vertical equity still remains largely one of value-judgment, but important new insights are being added by the new developments.

3. Applications to Income Taxation

I now turn to the application of these principles to some current issues of tax policy in the income tax field. These include (1) integration of the individual and corporation income taxes, (2) the treatment of capital gains, and (3) the nature of tax expenditures.

INTEGRATION

One of the most lively and stubborn issues of tax reform deals with the role of the corporation profit tax and its relation to the individual income tax. Two views of this relation may be taken: (1) corporate profits may be looked at as a proper source of taxation in their own right, distinct from and independent of the individual income tax; or (2) the corporation may be viewed as a conduit for capital income received by its owners, income which is to be included in the global income of the shareholders, and which is to be taxed uniformly under their individual income tax. The first view calls for an absolute or extra tax on corporate products. The second view calls for integration of corporate source income into the individual income tax base.

The principles of good tax structure provide no grounds for the first view. Ability to pay inherently relates to individuals, not legal institutions, and all income (as well as all taxes) must in the last resort be imputed to individuals. Corporation source income, therefore, should be taxed to the owner along with his income from all other sources, no more and no less. This does not rule out imposition of modest benefit charges on corporations, designed to pay for the cost of administering anti-trust or security market regulations, but such a charge would not take the form of a profits tax, nor would a tax designed for purposes of control (with regard to monopoly pricing or size) be of this form. Even if one accepts the proposition, finally, that the income tax should give more favorable treatment to earned income, this would not call for a corporation profits tax. Rather, it would call for an income tax surcharge on *all* capital income, including interest and profits from unincorporated enterprises as well as corporate profits. Finally, I should note that the case for integration, as just presented, rests on the assumption that the burden of the profits tax falls on profit or on capital income. But the case is not contingent on this assumption. If shifting into higher prices or lower wages occurs, the tax becomes a rather arbitrary form of product tax, much inferior to a general sales tax of the retail sales or value added type. Once more it becomes unacceptable, if for different reasons, as a part of the good tax system.

While it is evident, therefore, that there is no place for an absolute corporation profits tax in the good tax structure, it is nevertheless essential that retained earnings be included in the individual income tax base. Thus corporation profits remain a matter of tax concern. Full integration calls for imputing all corporate source earnings to the shareholder. Under this so-called partnership method, the corporation will advise the shareholders on amounts retained as well as dividends paid. In addition, it will serve as an agent of source withholding for the shareholder's individual income tax, just as it now serves as an agent for source withholding on taxes payable by its employees. But the tax thus collected from the corporation is then credited by the shareholder against his personal income tax.

As a less complete solution, integration may be limited to that part of profits which are distributed as dividends only. This may be done either by providing for a dividend received or a dividend paid credit. Under the former, the corporation tax is applied to all profits, but the shareholder is permitted, with appropriate grossing up, to credit the corporation tax already paid on his dividend income against his individual income tax. Under the dividend paid credit method, the corporation tax is applied to retained earnings only, while excluding dividends paid. Both methods secure correct integration for distributed profits only, but fail to do so with regard to retained earnings. Depending on whether the corporate rate falls short of or exceeds the marginal personal rate, shareholders will be under or over-taxed on the undistributed part of their corporate-source income. Of the two techniques the dividend-paid credit has the advantage of simplicity and also the merit of forestalling the possibility that the shareholder is permitted to credit a tax which in fact has been shifted to consumers. But, as noted below, considerations pertaining to the treatment of international capital income speak in favor of the dividend-received credit.

While the case for full integration is clear in principle, actual tax practice remains vacillating and confused. Most European countries have in recent years moved towards integration, at least in its partial (dividend-received credit) form and the U.S. and Canada are tending in the same direction. But most countries are as yet far short of accepting full integration as the proper solution. In part this reflects international aspects of tax policy, and in part the desire to hold on to a familiar and conveniently collected revenue source. It may also be argued that solution of the corporation tax problem must be related to the treatment of capital gains to which I now turn.

CAPITAL GAINS

Once more, the proper solution is clear in principle, but practice fails to comply with it. The point in principle is that accretion in the form of capital gains adds to the taxpayer's net worth no less than does accretion in other forms of income. Capital gains, therefore, should be taxed like other income. Moreover, it is irrelevant in this context whether gains are realized or not. Whether the property owner chooses to realize his gains or to hold them in accrued form is a matter of portfolio management which should be left to his discretion and which should have no bearing on his tax liability.

But though the principle is clear, its implementation meets with practical obstacles. Taxation of unrealized gains on an accrual basis requires current valuation. This is feasible for certain assets (such as traded shares) which carry a quoted market value but more difficult for others such as real estate. It has been suggested, therefore, that the former gains be taxed at reasonable intervals, say, every five years, while for the latter realization be deemed to occur at the time of transfer by bequest of gift. In this case, the taxpayer still stands to gain by the delay in tax payment, a defect which might be corrected by application of an interest charge. Given inclusion of unrealized gains into the tax base along these lines, the lock-in effect caused by full taxation of realized gains only is greatly reduced. At the same time, it would still be necessary to assure adequate averaging provisions. Otherwise, the discontinuous nature of capital gains would result in discriminatory treatment under a progressive rate structure.

While the good tax system calls for full taxation of capital gains, it also calls for a base adjustment so as to exclude inflationary gains. Income taxation, in the ability-to-pay or equal option context, must be related to real, not nominal income; and divergence between the real and nominal base is of particular importance with regard to capital gains. Regarding wage and salary income, inflation causes tax distortions only because of the progressive nature of the rate structure, and this may be handled readily by adjusting the nominal limits of bracket rates (be it through indexing or ad-hoc changes) in line with inflation. But proper treatment of capital gains requires the further step of base adjustment, and would do so even under a flat rate or proportional tax. A doubling of nominal values while prices double leaves no real gain so that an inflation adjustment of the base is needed. At the same time, the adjustment should be symmetrical. If, for instance, depreciation is placed on a replacement-cost basis so as to allow for inflation, there should also be an adjustment for gains which result as the real value of indebtedness is reduced. Once more, the principle of capital gains treatment is clear enough but actual practice is a different matter. The U.S., Canada and the U.K. now tax realized gains, though at more or less preferential rates, while disregarding unrealized gains. Most continental countries, including Belgium, do even less in reaching full capital gains taxation. The main reason, I suppose, is that the nominal level of rate structures is more progressive than legislatures in fact mean them to be, thus making preferential treatment of capital gains a not-too-visible means by which to dampen the impact of the statutory rate structures. Clearly it would be preferable from the point of view of tax structure design to accept a full income base, and then to adjust rates downward so as to bring them in line with what is considered to be acceptable.

Another reason for reluctance to tax capital gains fully is concern over the consequences for capital formation and growth. Undoubtedly, full taxation of capital gains would increase the tax burden on capital income and thus might have detrimental growth effects. But this is not a convincing defense of the preferential gains treatment. If allowance is to be made for growth incentives, it should be done in the most efficient manner and so as to interfere least with equity considerations. Preferential capital gains treatment, therefore, must be compared with alternative incentive techniques such as the investment credit or initial write-offs which, I suggest, are superior devices to deal with the problem.

TAX EXPENDITURES

This leads me to the broader issue of tax loopholes, preferences and incentives. It is estimated in the United States that the current tax base could be increased by about one-third if all special provisions and tax preferences were eliminated. Thus, the same revenue could be obtained by a substantially reduced level of tax rates. This would moderate interference with economic decisions, improve tax equity and present a more honest picture of tax burden distribution. High bracket rates could be lowered without, in effect, reducing the progressivity of the actual tax burden distribution.

Another way of looking at this problem is to view the tax reductions which result from the granting of various tax preferences as subsidies or "tax expenditures."[3] Thus, preferential treatment of home owners in the United States (due to deductibility of mortgage interest without inclusion of imputed rent of owner-occupied housing) may be considered as a subsidy to housing, faster than economic depreciation may be viewed as a subsidy to investment, exemption of interest on state and local securities may be viewed as a subsidy to state-local borrowing, deductibility of charitable contributions may be viewed as a subsidy to churches and educational institutions, and so forth. These subsidies may thus be viewed as matching grants to various types of economic activity. Since the benefit is typically given as a deduction from income, the matching rate granted will depend on the taxpayer's marginal bracket rate. The question then is whether the government would be willing to undertake such expenditures and in that particular form, if they were to be made in explicit fashion and financed through expenditure appropriations. Explicit subsidy payments would be a more above-board way of dealing with expenditure programs; and by requiring them to be handled by appropriation committees, which have more expertise in particular expenditure lines (e.g., supports for housing) a more efficient expenditure program should result. As a step in this direction, the U.S. budget is now required to list the cost of such "tax-expenditures" and to specify the expenditure categories of the budget under which they should be included.

While this is a useful innovation, it must be kept in mind that the concept of "tax-expenditure" is a derived one only. To determine what *is* a tax expenditure, we must first determine what is the proper tax base, and not vice-versa. Moreover, proper definition of the tax base not only calls for inclusion of all items that should be included, but it also calls for exclusion of items that should be excluded. Thus, if there are "tax-expenditures" which result from these omissions, there are also "expenditure taxes" which result from excessive inclusions. However, the former clearly exceed the latter, leaving the question to what extent the tax system should be used to implement subsidy policies. In a perfectly rational setting, it would, of course, be a matter of indifference whether subsidy policies are handled separately or whether they are netted out against tax payments. But in practice the results will differ greatly depending on whether expenditure policies are determined directly or are permitted to be imbedded implicitly into tax provisions. As noted in my first lecture, there is a strong case for arguing that the decision process will be more efficient if a distinction is drawn between separate policy issues.

4. *Application to Other Taxes*

I now leave the central problem of income taxation and turn briefly to other components of the tax structure.

TAXES ON WEALTH

In the context of an ability-to-pay system, where ability is measured by income, there is no need for an additional tax on wealth. Such a tax may be seen as a tax on capital income, but capital income is already included in a properly defined income base. Thus, bequests or gifts should be included in a full accretion base, as should be income derived in imputed rather than in cash form. To the extent that this is not the case, a tax on wealth, however, may serve to correct deficiencies in the income tax.

The taxation of wealth on a current basis should be distinguished from that of death duties. The rationale for death duties is related to society's desire to limit the right of transfer at death or to control the concentration of wealth, both objectives which differ from and may be supplementary to the role of income taxation.

COMMODITY TAXES

There is room for debate, in the context of an ability to pay or equal option-based model of the good tax system, whether the base should be viewed in terms of income (accretion) or consumption. But it is clear that whichever of the two bases is chosen, it should be applied in the context of a personal tax, with allowance for the size of the taxpaying unit and for a rate structure which depends upon the taxpayer's global base. Both the income tax and a personal-type expenditure tax meet this principle, but *in rem* taxes (whether in the general form of a retail sales tax or value added tax, or in the form of selected excises) do not. Yet such taxes continue to provide a large and perhaps growing share of total revenue in most tax systems. How is this to be judged as a matter of tax structure design?

Consider first the role of a general retail sales tax or its equivalent, a consumption type value added tax, which (in line with European practice) excludes capital goods from its base. Such a tax rests on a more or less global consumption base, but it fails to allow for family size and it excludes application of progressive rates to a global base. This leaves it inferior to a personal type expenditure or consumption tax. To some extent, these disadvantages may be compensated for by family allowances and by viewing it as supplementary to the progressive income tax. Another difference, sometimes cited in favor of the sales tax, is its lesser visibility to the taxpayer, but I would consider this a deficiency rather than an advantage. Returning to what I have said earlier about the benefit approach, taxes should be visible, not hidden. Only then can they serve a meaningful role in the political process of budget determination. Selective excises are frequently defended as means of penalizing undesirable forms of consumption, i.e. "demerit goods". While justification of typically regressive liquor and tobacco taxes on these grounds seems questionable, the use of selective taxes on luxury goods may serve as a useful if second best way of applying a progressive expenditure tax. In particular, such taxation of luxury goods may play a highly constructive role in the tax system of developing countries, where a personal expenditure tax is well beyond the bounds of administrative feasibility.

Next, selective excises may be used as a means of minimizing the efficiency costs of taxation. As mentioned earlier, one of the difficulties of implementing an equal options tax is failure to include leisure in the tax base. Thus selective excises placed on products which are complementary to leisure may offer a way of approximating the taxation of leisure itself. Finally, selective commodity taxes may be useful in internalizing social costs (e.g., pollution or crowding) thereby serving an efficiency objective. The European practice, perhaps soon to be followed in the United States, of taxing automobiles in line with engine size, is a good illustration. For these and other reasons it would be incorrect to exclude selective excises from the good tax structure, even though they do not readily fit the requirement of horizontal and vertical equity considerations.

PAYROLL TAX

We must not, in this review of major tax bases, pass over the payroll tax. Along with the rise of the transfer share in budget expenditures, noted in my first lecture, the share of payroll taxes in total revenue has increased greatly. Such taxes are typically imposed at a flat rate and without exemption, but they tend to be regressive in terms of total income. This is the case since wage income tends to decline as a share of total income when moving up the income scale. Moreover, this tendency is strengthened if there is a ceiling to the amount of wage income which is to be included in the taxable base.

Viewed by itself, the payroll tax appears a rather archaic appendix to the income tax. There is little ground on which to argue that there should be an additional and flat rate tax on wage income only. The crucial question, however, is whether the payroll tax should be viewed in this way or whether it should be considered as part of a social security system. If such a system

68

was operated on an actuarial basis, the combined payroll tax and benefit effect would become distributionally neutral. Reality as usual lies between these two extremes. On the one hand, modern social security systems diverge substantially from a *quid-pro-quo* basis. On the other, it is evident that the rise of payroll taxation has occurred in conjunction with the expansion of social security benefits, thus providing some basis for viewing the two in conjunction. Given this perspective, an argument may be made for retaining the payroll tax as the core basis of finance supported by a general budgetary contribution where redistributional considerations so require.

5. Initial Tax Design vs. Tax Reform

The preceding discussion has examined which taxes should or should not be included in the "good" tax structure. But there is a difference between the problem of designing a tax structure *de novo* and that of tax reform, i.e. of adjusting an already existing tax structure. Unfortunately, it is the latter with which ongoing policy must deal. The point is that existing differential taxes have become capitalized, so that their replacement by a general tax does not remove old inequities. If in the past a tax was imposed on asset x held by investor A, the value of that asset was reduced. When, subsequently, the asset was purchased by B, a lower price was paid, so as to leave the burden with A. Thus there remains no horizontal inequity between B and investor C who holds a tax-free asset Y. On the contrary, removal of the partial tax will grant a windfall to B as the price of x rises, thus compounding rather than correcting the state of horizontal inequity.

This being the case, is tax reform worthwhile, or is it merely a vain attempt to eradicate the "original sin" of past errors?[4] This is a significant question, but I do not think that it should dampen the zest for tax reform. For one thing, unjustified gains which resulted in the process of restoring neutrality may be dealt with by capital gains taxation. For another, broadening the base remains desirable on efficiency grounds, even though past iniquities are not removed. Finally, the difficulty which is based on the capitalization of tax differentials arises only in the taxation of assets but does not pertain to other potential aspects of tax reform such as the income tax rate structure, the base of a sales tax and other features of the tax structure which are not compensated for by a process of capitalization.

6. International Aspects

It remains to note how these considerations of good tax structure are qualified if examined in an open-economy setting where international trade and capital movements occur. As noted in my earlier lectures, this aspect of the fiscal problem, though relatively novel, will continue to gain in importance. At the least, this poses the question of how international transactions are to be handled in national tax structures; and ultimately, it may call for the design of an international fiscal system.

INCOME TAXATION

Beginning with the taxation of income, two major problems arise. One is how a country should tax the foreign source income of its own residents; and the other is how a country should tax the income of foreigners originating within its jurisdiction.[5]

Foreign Source Income of Residents. The problem of taxing foreign source income of residents (persons or corporations) can be approached in two ways. One way is to take an international view of equity, holding that residents with similar amounts of income should pay the same *total* tax (domestic plus foreign) independent of how their income is divided between local and foreign sources. To accomplish this, the foreign tax must be credited against the domestic tax and, if the former is higher, a refund must be paid. Another way is to take a national view of equity, requiring taxpayers with similar income to pay the same amount of *domestic* tax. This calls for treating the foreign tax as a deduction from income.

Either view may be defended on equity grounds, but they differ in efficiency terms. The international view (credit method) leads to an efficient allocation of capital resources on a world-wide basis, since tax considerations are made neutral in choosing the country in which one wishes to invest one's funds. The national view (deduction method) leads to efficient allocation in the national sense. That is to say, foreign investment will now be carried to a point where returns from foreign investment net of foreign tax are equalized with returns from domestic investment including the domestic tax.

There is the further question of *when* foreign income should be taxed, a matter which is of major importance in connection with foreign subsidiaries or multinationals. Usual practice is for the country of residence to tax such income only at the time of repatriation, i.e., to defer the domestic tax until then. In situations where the foreign tax is lower, this involves an incentive to foreign investment and, in particular, to foreign investment in low (tax-haven) jurisdictions. Under either the national or international perspective, deferral seems an inappropriate procedure.

Income of Foreigners within Jurisdiction. Turning to the other side of the coin, the question is how a country should tax the income accruing to foreign residents but originating within its jurisdiction. All countries claim the right to tax such income, which is reasonable enough, but at what rates? Thus an important new dimension is added to the equity problem – i.e., how should the claim to international tax bases be distributed among nations?

The answer given under the non-discrimination rule is that the rate should be the same as applies to residents. This rule is readily applicable under the corporation tax where a flat rate is used, but interpretation is difficult under the income tax. If x, a resident of country A, derives income in both countries A and B, should B apply a rate pertaining to his earnings in B only, or should his entire income be considered? In the case of capital income originating in B, should B apply its corporation tax only, or should it be entitled also to a personal income tax on dividends when received by the foreign shareholder? Such seems to be the objective when the country of origin applies a withholding tax at the time of repatriation, yet this tax is typically credited against the corporation tax in the country of residence rather than passed through to the individual shareholder.

All this has substantial bearing on the previously considered problem of integration. Full integration will result in the loss of revenue base to the country of origin unless a withholding tax is used to partake in the personal income tax in the country of residence. Partial integration via exclusion of dividends from the corporation tax has a similar result, while partial integrating via crediting at the shareholder level does not. It is not surprising, therefore, that capital importing countries, such as Canada and U.K. have opted for the latter method, and this is also the goal of Common Market policy.

Finally, there is the difficult question of deciding just where income originates. In many instances, foreign investment income involves more than one country and there is no simple rule (such as the so-called "arms length" procedure) by which to decide the issue. As noted in my first lecture, the growing internationalization of property ownership and capital flows renders it increasingly difficult to tax capital income at the national level. This suggests that the good tax system of the future may have to tax international capital incomes through an international system. Revenue allocation in such a system, moreover, may come to play a significant role in dealing with the problem of international income distribution.

Turning to the treatment of commodity taxes in the international system, a two-fold distinction must be drawn. One is between taxes which are imposed at the point of origin (production) and those which are imposed at the point of destination (consumption). The other is between taxes which are general and taxes which are selective. Moreover, the appropriate treatment differs depending on whether the problem is viewed in a system of fixed or flexible exchange rates.

When the GATT system was established, the former was the case. Hence export rebates were allowed on origin taxes (selective or global) thereby transforming them into destination taxes and voiding the occurrence of trade or balance of payments effects. In the current setting of more flexible exchange rates, there is no need for border tax adjustments in relation to general type origin taxes, since exchange rate adjustments will compensate for resulting changes in cost. A need for border adjustments (export rebates and compensating import duties) continues, however, for the case of selective type consumption taxes. Since a similar adjustment for general taxes does no harm (even though it is not needed) I see no reason why the former GATT rule should not be continued even in the flexible exchange rate setting.

TAX INTEGRATION

I conclude with a word about tax integration and its relation to tax equalization. If tax integration is defined as removing distorting effects which result from the coexistence of separate tax systems, integration can be accomplished, through appropriate rebate and compensating duty devices, without having to equalize tax rates between countries. Equalization is needed only if it is desired as an objective in its own right, or if the administrative complexities involved in integration (i.e., in making border adjustments) are to be avoided. This, I take it, is the major objective of equalization of tax rates for the value added and subsequently for the corporation income tax in the Common Market. In addition, it may serve to simplify the allocation of tax shares in a common community budget. Once more, the international aspects become an increasingly important factor in tax structure design. They will modify the principle of good tax structure which we have examined, but there will remain the basic problem of how to distribute taxes in an equitable fashion and with least cost to the efficiency of the economic system.

1 / For the basic statement see Henry Simons, *Personal Income Taxation*, Chicago, University of Chicago Press, 1938.

2 / For a convenient summary see A. Sandmo, "Optimal Taxation – An Introduction to the Literature," *Journal of Public Economics*, January 1975.

3 / See Stanley S. Surrey, *Pathways to Tax Reform*, Cambridge, Mass, Harvard, 1973.

4 / See R.A. Musgrave, *The Theory of Public Finance*, McGraw-Hill, 1958, p. 38. For a recent development of the argument see M. Feldstein, "On the Theory of Tax Reform," *Journal of Public Economics*, July 1976.

5 / See R.A. Musgrave, *Fiscal Systems*, Part III, New Haven, Conn., Yale 1969.

2

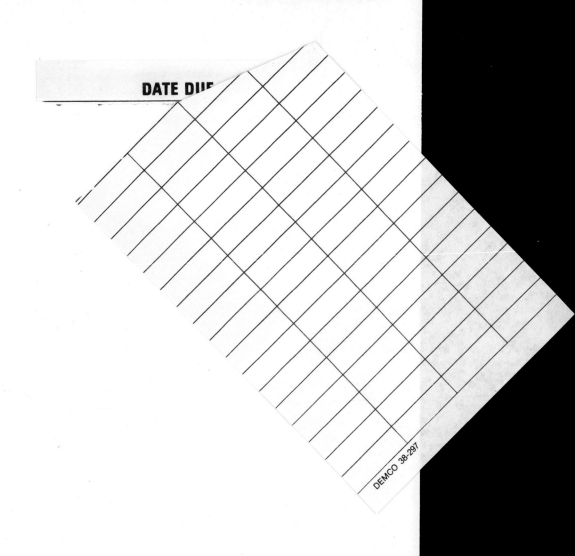

DATE DUE

DEMCO 38-297